Stewardship Economy   1

private property without private ownership

Julian Pratt

First edition 2011

Second edition 2021

The moral right of the author has been asserted

Published by

To order a paperback copy go to http://stewardship-economy.org/stewardship-economy/or www.lulu.com

ISBN 9-78471-703140

Contents

Acknowledgements

I owe a huge debt of gratitude to John Kemp, who introduced me to these ideas nearly half a century ago and continues to provoke interesting conversations.

Most of my family, friends, acquaintances and many passers-by have been drawn into conversations about land ownership and I thank them all for their forbearance and questioning, which has shaped my thinking. I remember my son Richard and daughter Eleanor who, asking the 'why' questions that young children ask, learned to respond to my deep in breath in preparation for a reply with a quick 'it's all right, Dad, we know – it all comes down to land ownership'.

I'd particularly like to thank Seán Boyle for discussions about modelling the transition to stewardship, Eleanor Field for her suggestions about presenting environmental economics, Anne and Pete Gillies for helping me to see that this material could be of interest to the general reader, Pat Gordon for her encouragement and ideas about presentation, Alan Gorman for many interesting talks and for the metaphor of the railway carriage and Richard Pethen for encouraging me to use my personal story.

In the production phase I'd like to thank Keith Povey Editorial Services, and particularly Marilyn Hamshere, for editorial assistance – you, too, can thank them that this book is now half its original length. Thanks, too, to Kathryn Banner for yet another wonderful design, this time for the book cover for the first edition.

Of quite another order of magnitude are my thanks to my wife Rosemary Field who has done everything possible to encourage and support me to write what I needed to write, from wielding her sharp editorial pencil to providing me with all I have needed to live my dream. Thank you, Rosie.

In these times of cuts to state funding I am particularly reminded that none of this writing would have been possible without access to source material through libraries that provide free access to the public. I should particularly like to thank the British Library, the library of the London School of Economics and Political Science, the City of Sheffield libraries and the City of Westminster libraries, and their ever-helpful staff.

I'd like to thank the following writers and publishers for permission to reprint copyright material:

Page 39. Robb Johnson (2000) *Margaret Thatcher: my part in her downfall* – an aside from his wonderful song *When 6B go swimming* reproduced with thanks to Robb Johnson.

Page 130. Fred Harrison (2006) *Ricardo's Law: house prices and the great tax clawback scam* – quotation reproduced with thanks to Shepheard-Walwyn.

Julian Pratt
London
February 2011

Editor's note: Second edition

In the first edition of this book Julian pointed to supplementary work that he intended to publish. Sadly, he died before he was able to complete this. Even so, much of the material is well developed, so it seems worth making it available to anyone for whom it may be of interest. This is published as books 2-7, with this summary book as the first in the series.

Some of the examples Julian provides in this and the other books are out of date and some references are not available. I hope you, the reader, will excuse this and will find the work as a whole thought-provoking and topical.

Julian published the first edition of *Stewardship Economy* in 2011 and continued to develop the ideas until his death in 2018. He would, I'm sure, wish to add to the list of acknowledgements those who contributed and challenged him during these years – colleagues and dear friends with whom he had many lively conversations and whose views he respected deeply. They include members of the Henry George Foundation, the Labour Land Campaign, the Liberal Democrat ALTER group, and, in particular, Gareth Whelan, Jonty Williams, Justin Robbins and Gavin Kerr. Thank you all.

Rosemary Field

September 2021

Books in the series

Stewardship Economy 1: private property without private ownership is the first book and provides an overall summary of the main ideas.

Stewardship Economy 2: Valuing land and managing transition sets out in some detail how to establish the market rent of land and how to make the transition from an ownership to a stewardship economy. It also considers how the revenue from stewardship fees might be distributed.

Stewardship Economy 3: Land, environment and climate explores how a stewardship economy would transform the way we use land, provide housing and develop our cities. It goes on to consider how stewardship would help address pressing environmental and climate concerns.

Stewardship Economy 4: The economy, wealth and universal income focuses on the impact of stewardship on the national and global economy, how the distribution of wealth would be changed and the impact of a Universal Income.

Stewardship Economy 5: efficient, fair taxes and the role of the state describes the some of the adverse effects of our current system of taxation and considers the role of the state in a stewardship economy. It also explains some basic economic principles and terms.

Stewardship Economy 6: property rights describes the systems of property rights in our current economic system, their history and how property rights could be more fair and efficient in a stewardship economy.

Stewardship Economy 7: some economics explained, economic terms and bibliography. This book provides an introduction to some key economic concepts for the non-specialist and lists the references for all the books, as far as they are available.

Part I Approaches to Stewardship

Part I offers three approaches to stewardship:

Chapter 1, the Introduction, includes a brief summary of stewardship and an overview of the structure of the book.

Chapter 2 describes how I became interested in stewardship. Sometimes a story is the best way in.

Chapter 3 takes as examples the radio spectrum and climate change and shows how stewardship in all but name is already being applied to their management.

Start with whichever chapter draws you in. This Part I will enable you to judge whether this is a book you want to read.

If your response to anything you read takes the form of 'Yes, but...' it would be worth checking out the Frequently Answered Questions section of this book, as you are not alone.

Chapter 1 Introduction

Stewardship economy

I have written *Stewardship Economy: Private property without private ownership* for the broadsheet reader who is looking for a new lens through which to view the major economic issues of our time – poverty, inequalities, the environment, globalisation, the tax-benefit system, pensions, house prices, negative equity, banking, recession, unemployment, sovereign debt ….

The lens I offer is the property system that we apply to the natural world.

Markets require an underpinning institutional framework, including property rights and an enforceable law of contract, if they are to function. Our ideas about property are so fundamental to our economy and society that we rarely question them. I don't question the role of market mechanisms themselves, or the role of the state in regulating the economy and providing public goods. I do, however, question the most fundamental element of the institutional framework: the system of property rights.

The system of property rights with which we are most familiar, ownership, serves us well enough for things that people have produced (artefacts) – chairs, cars, houses and so on. But it serves us poorly when we apply it to the natural world – land and the environment. These terms, and others used in this book, are defined in the Glossary.

I use the term 'ownership economy' to refer to the sort of economy with which we are familiar, in which the natural world can be owned.

What would it be like to live in a society that does not treat the land and the environment as things that can be owned in the same way as things that people have made? I am not proposing any change in the ownership of artefacts, or for collective or common property rights to the natural world. But I am proposing a new form of private property that we can apply to the natural world.

I use the term 'stewardship' to describe a private property system that is similar to ownership, but different in several ways:

The steward of a part of the natural world has
- o *the right of access* – to use it in the way that they choose, within the constraints of any relevant regulations
- o *the responsibility of care* – to manage it responsibly and husband it for future generations, accepting liability for any damage done to it
- o *the duty of compensation* – to pay an annual fee, equal to its market rent, into a fund that is used to benefit everyone
- o *ownership*, in the conventional sense, of any buildings or other improvements.

A 'stewardship economy' is one in which the natural world is held in stewardship, while artefacts are held in ownership.

In a stewardship economy the annual fees for the use of land, stewardship fees, provide a fund of income that may be distributed to the whole population as a Universal Income – an income (which may be age-related) paid to everybody unconditionally without means test or work requirement. Or the fund may replace conventional taxes as a source of revenue for the state.

Environmental charges provide an income that is distributed on an equal per capita basis as an Environmental Dividend or invested for the benefit of future generations.

The context

Over the last two centuries market-based economies, along with cheap energy and technological change, have played a key role in transforming the quality of life for billions of people. But the problems of these economies, even at the best of times, are well-rehearsed – in particular, the persistence of poverty and inequality with their associated ill-health and squandering of human potential; environmental damage; and the suffering caused by unemployment and economic recessions.

Responses to these problems have included proposals for a wide range of interventions including redistributive taxation, environmental taxation and a lesser – or greater – role for the state.

Since the fall of the Berlin Wall in 1989, if not before, most people have not found it credible that a complex economy can be managed by central planning. Since the failure of the global financial system in 2008, if not before, most people have not found it credible that the economy can be left to unregulated free markets.

The question that now needs extensive debate could be framed as: 'What is the appropriate legal and regulatory framework within which markets should operate?' Property rights are an essential element of this institutional framework.

Now is the right time to think about the fundamental underpinnings of the economy. We have all, since 2007, had to learn far more about the workings of the global financial system than we ever really wanted to know, so we are well prepared to delve into the assumptions that lie deep within our economic system. And as one nation after another struggles with the problem of sovereign debt, innovative ways of raising revenue deserve thorough investigation.

The book

Stewardship Economy: Private property without private ownership makes five major contributions:

(i) I advocate *a new form of private property in land, which I call stewardship, and which is fairer than ownership and allocates land more efficiently* (Chapters 6 & 12). The land is held in trust for all people; the steward of a plot of land pays an annual stewardship fee that is equal to its market rent; and the fees collected are either used as revenue for the state (substituting for at least some conventional taxation) or distributed to everyone as Universal Income.

(ii) I propose that *the environment – air, oceans, rivers, electromagnetic spectrum and so on – also be held in trust for all people.* Where environmental resources are scarce they are allocated to stewards who pay an annual fee for the privilege of using them; and the revenue is distributed as an Environmental Dividend or invested for the benefit of future generations (Chapters 7 & 12).

(iii) I describe *what it would be like to live in an established stewardship economy, where 100 per cent of the market rent of land is collected for the benefit of us all* (Part III). Various sorts of taxes on land have been proposed in ownership economies as solutions to particular problems, such as improving land use or funding transport infrastructure. It may seem least risky to address each of these problems in isolation. But stewardship offers a single intervention that brings multiple crosscutting benefits to most areas of social and economic life. My purpose is to describe the wide range of these benefits so that it is possible to see the whole picture. I hope that this description of a stewardship economy makes it easier to imagine taking the first steps towards such a future.

(iv) I tackle the question of *how to collect the whole of the market rent without distorting the efficient allocation of land* (Chapter 13). This has its own challenges, and these are not illuminated by the valuable theory and practice that has been developed for Land Value Tax levied at up to 50 per cent of market rents.

(v) I also describe *a clear mechanism for transition from an ownership economy to a stewardship economy, which treats existing landowners fairly* (Chapter 14). I suggest that, during transition, the annual fee should be equal to any *increase* in market rent that occurs after the onset of transition. However, over time, probably decades, the market value (purchase price) of land that remains in private hands will tend towards zero.

Stewardship ensures that everybody benefits when a person or other legal entity holds the monopoly right to access part of the natural world. It is closely associated with proposals to ensure that the revenue generated by other monopoly rights, such as the right to issue money, flow to the community not to individuals or corporations (Chapter 8).

Timeliness

Home owners find it difficult to view stewardship positively during times of rising house prices but find it easier to recognise its advantages when they are reminded that house prices can fall.

Stewardship is highly relevant to the circumstances of 2011. Among its many advantages, it:

o   offers the only certain way of preventing the sort of house price bubble that led to the sub-prime mortgage scandal of 2007 and the subsequent credit crunch, bank failures and recession

o   ensures that nobody faces negative equity due to a fall in land prices

o   provides a source of revenue that could reduce the budget deficit and sovereign debt

o   offers a way to help support the unemployed back into work

o   provides everybody with an income stream that compensates an average energy user for rising energy prices.

Readership

You're particularly likely to be interested if you are interested in any of the following:

o   how to eradicate absolute poverty, reduce inequalities and social exclusion and achieve distributive justice

- o the problem of sovereign debt and how to cut the budget deficit
- o how a market economy could create more wealth
- o the welfare state, pension provision and the perverse impact of the tax-benefit system on employment
- o sustainability, and how economic instruments that protect the environment could be made fairer and so more politically acceptable
- o self-financing transport infrastructure
- o land reform.

Structure

Stewardship Economy: Private property without private ownership provides an overview of a stewardship economy. It describes:

- o approaches to stewardship (Part I)
- o stewardship in essence (Part II)
- o stewardship in practice (Part III)
- o stewardship – why and how? (Part IV)
- o transition to stewardship (Part V)
- o opportunities and challenges (Part VI)
- o frequently answered questions.

The first four parts focus almost exclusively on the description of an established, steady-state, stewardship economy. This approach is Utopian – not in the derogatory sense of 'indulging in impracticably ideal projects for social welfare' but in the sense of describing an ideal as a prelude to describing very practical ways of getting there. Unlike many Utopian texts it does not assume a perfected humanity, communal property rights, a planned or predetermined economy or fantasies of material abundance. It prescribes nothing apart from a very specific change in the property system for land and the environment, and the distribution of the market rent of that natural property. Just as in the Utopia of a society from which slavery has been abolished, only one thing has changed; yet everything has changed.

You might prefer a historical approach, starting with an analysis of a modern economy and moving on to proposals to reform it. But at times this historical approach limits how radically we can think. One way to avoid this limitation is to describe a desired future and only then to map out the path that would have been followed if one had got there.

That is the approach taken in *Stewardship Economy: Private property without private ownership.* It is only in Part V that I look at how, where and when it might be possible to make the transition from ownership to stewardship.

Stewardship Economy: Private property without private ownership (Parts III – V) is a summary of material contained in the additional books. For the detail behind this book, please look at the other work (books 2-7 in the series).

Chapter 2   My interest in stewardship

In the 1970s I worked in a hospital in the Eastern Cape in South Africa. Most deaths were caused by under-nutrition and infectious diseases – diseases of poverty. People lived by subsistence agriculture, eked out with small sums of money sent home by migrant workers at the mines. Apart from a small number of commercial farms, owned by white people, the land was overpopulated, overgrazed and eroded.

The right of access – who gets to use the natural world?

I found myself thinking about the causes of poverty while living in an agricultural society. While some of my contemporaries in England were questioning the ownership of the means of production, my attention was focused more narrowly on the ownership and use of the land.

Redrawing the boundaries between states

This focus was unavoidable because, at that time, the apartheid government of South Africa was imposing its policy of the 'homelands', including the part of the Eastern Cape that it called Transkei. This was part of a programme to institutionalise the existing allocation of land in the republic. Under the Natives 'Land Act of 1913, black people had been barred from owning land outside these 'homeland' areas – allocating less than 13 per cent of the land area to more than 75 per cent of the population.

The boundary of Transkei had been drawn to include a land area that was too small for its population. It didn't include any significant mineral resources or harbours. No matter how much capital was invested it would never be in a position to open a port or develop a mining industry, as it lacked the necessary natural resources.

The apartheid government was imposing its decision about which land would be available to be owned by white people and which by black people. I could see, in South Africa more clearly than back in England, that land ownership is ultimately based on the exercise of power. Although the ownership of land in England is transferred by voluntary contract, the sequence of contracts can, in principle, always be traced back to some historical moment when the land was taken by force or the prerogative of the state – even though this may mean looking as far back as the enclosures, the dissolution of the monasteries or the Norman conquest.

Land reform

I wondered what a post-apartheid government could do if it had a mandate to embark on a programme of land reform – redistributing land from large landowners to those who work and live on the land.

Simply dividing the land into equal plots could have serious disadvantages – parcelling up a viable commercial farm and handing it over to small farmers with little capital would be likely to cause a fall in production. And even if a fair distribution of land could be achieved in the short term, it would simply create a new class of landowners and a new group of the excluded. How could it remain fair for generations into the future – particularly as the population grew? What about urban and industrial land? What about the ownership of natural resources?

I could not imagine that simply redistributing land by a further exercise of power would produce efficient land use or lasting solutions. And it would require either large amounts of state money to buy out the existing farmers or coercion. Rather than pursuing the rather limited goal of transferring ownership from one group to another, I began to wonder whether we should be challenging the very nature of ownership itself.

An alternative to ownership of land

I had always taken it for granted that land could be owned in the same way as anything else. But in Transkei land was allocated locally by the tribal chief, at least partly on the basis of need and the ability to use it. This form of property recognised that all members of the community had a right to use the land, but not to own it outright.

These customary arrangements draw on traditional land tenure systems but were institutionalised by the colonial powers, which chose to recognise certain cultural (tribal) groups as indigenous and forcibly re-located them to designated territories or 'homelands'. This system of tribal authority has resulted throughout Africa in protracted conflicts between the 'indigenous' and those outsiders who cross tribal boundaries (Mahmood Mamdani 2011:31). Even within the tribe this system gives a great deal of personal power to the chief and may prevent the successful from accumulating and working more land, discouraging improvement and investment.

But these arrangements opened up new possibilities for me, seeing in operation an approach to land ownership that was different from those I knew about from Europe and the Soviet Union. It was not that it was better, but that seeing one alternative in operation gave me permission to think about others. And as Fred Harrison (2008:51) has pointed out, this culture of common property in land has provided the basis for the collection of resource rents by the state – for example Botswana's Mines and Minerals Act (1967), which has vested subsoil mineral rights in the state and laid the foundations for one of the most successful economies in sub-Saharan Africa.

What would happen if you separated the financial benefit of owning land from the practical benefits of using it? Suppose that everybody in Transkei – or, more radically, everybody in South Africa – paid rent for their land; and that this revenue was shared out equally amongst everybody living there. This would achieve the underlying purpose of land reform, of providing everybody with a share in the wealth of the land, without requiring any change in who actually occupies and uses it. Where a large commercial farm was the most productive way of using the land it would continue to operate as before, but everybody would receive a share of the rent paid by its occupier. Where subsistence farming was the best use it would continue; but where it was not, people could surrender their land and avoid any liability to pay rent while still receiving their share of the pooled rent of all the land. Paying a charge for the use of land and distributing the revenue to everybody offers the possibility of a peaceful and affordable route to land reform.

The responsibility of care – sustainable development

But what about the way that land and the environment are treated?

In South Africa, in the nearby Valley of a Thousand Hills, Dr Halley Stott had adopted an inspirational approach to holistic health and social care through the Valley Trust and supported by Oxfam. They had set up demonstration gardens that relied not on irrigation and fertilisers but on composting and deep trenching. They provided local people with small loans, which were repaid from the sale of their produce, for the fencing materials needed to keep the goats away. In the dry season, these gardens stood out as oases of green dotted over the hills. What a contrast with Transkei, where the earth was bare, baked and eroded. When the rains came to us, the rivers ran heavy with topsoil and the sea turned brown for miles from each river mouth.

This made me very aware of the fragility of the environment, particularly the few inches of topsoil that sustain life on Earth. And it led me to think about the incentives that property and financial systems do, or do not, provide to manage the natural world in a sustainable way.

The duty of compensation – distributive justice

When I returned to the UK and post-industrial Sheffield the pattern of ill health and death was, of course, dramatically different from that in South Africa. There is little serious under-nutrition and few lethal acute infectious diseases, while ill-health and premature death are dominated by cardiovascular disease, cancers and accidents. These are related to relative poverty, to people having an income that does not allow them to participate in the life of the community, rather than to absolute measures of poverty (Peter Townsend and Nick Davidson 1982:175).

My immediate interest shifted away from the ownership of the natural world to the way that our economy currently distributes the wealth it creates, and why this feels so unfair.

There are many causes of inequality – differences in inherited wealth, opportunities for education and training, and the complex mix of factors that have been described as social exclusion. It's easy to see the importance of employment (or self-employment) in reducing exclusion and inequalities. It is, however, difficult to believe either that full employment is likely over a long time frame in an ownership economy; or that it could provide a complete solution to inequalities, given the vast and increasing pay differentials between the highest and lowest paid. It is essential that some form of transfer payment is made to those who are not in work for a variety of reasons (such as sickness, unemployment, pregnancy, education, youth and old age), and to those in low-paid work. I had daily experience with the well-rehearsed problems of our Beveridge-style benefit system – inadequate benefit levels, humiliating assessments, low take-up, perverse incentives not to work, resentful taxpayers and so on. And I could see how Child Benefit largely avoids these problems.

Child Benefit is paid directly to the person responsible for each child without any exclusions. An unconditional benefit of this sort is criticised by economists on the grounds that it requires the collection of more tax than does a targeted, means-tested, benefit; and by politicians, in search of ways to cut costs, on the grounds that it rewards middle-income and high-income people unnecessarily. It has, however, quite widespread support because it is paid to the right person at the right time without the intrusiveness, poor uptake and hassle of means-tested benefits; as well as binding the middle class into the benefit system in a way that prevents them from demonising the recipients.

A suggested reform to the benefits system is the Citizen's Income or Basic Income (Hermione Parker, 1989: 127), the proposal to pay a guaranteed unconditional, non-withdrawable income to each individual without means test or work requirement – the equivalent of Child Benefit for all. This would provide everybody with a small independent income that would be particularly helpful in times of ill health, unemployment, retirement and so on. People would be able to top it up from savings and from whatever work they were able to find, whether high- or low-paid, full- or part-time. There would be nothing to discourage them from working.

When people describe Citizen's Income in this way they usually anticipate that it would be funded from general taxation, in particular from Income Tax. This arrangement would mean that, even if Citizen's Income were to be introduced, it could not be generous and there would be a constant struggle to raise the taxes needed to fund it.

I wondered whether in the UK a charge on land values, as proposed in Transkei for entirely different reasons, could provide the basis for funding a Citizen's Income. Indeed, it seemed possible that such a charge might also produce enough revenue to substitute for conventional taxes.

Charges on land values and the distribution of a guaranteed unconditional income to everybody are the central features of a stewardship economy.

This is not as big a leap as you might think. We already have experience of allocating access to an aspect of the environment – part of the radio spectrum – by requiring its users to pay a charge.

Chapter 3   Current examples

The ideas that underpin stewardship are widely accepted in mainstream discussions of how best to manage the environment.

This chapter introduces two examples. The first describes the way in which radio spectrum for mobile phones has been successfully allocated in many countries. The second describes a well-known proposal for the management of greenhouse gas emissions. Both are examples of stewardship in all but name.

Radio spectrum

When you want to receive a radio signal, you tune the receiver to the frequency of the station you are interested in. The best way to prevent interference using currently available technology is for each station to use a different frequency on the spectrum.

In the 1920s radio stations mushroomed in the USA and interference between their signals led the government to set up a Federal Radio Commission with the responsibility of issuing licences to broadcasters. These licences, allocating the exclusive (monopoly) right to use some part of the radio spectrum, were gifted to the stations. When the spectrum is allocated in this way, without making a charge, this gift from the state contributes to the radio stations 'profits but fails to ensure that they make good use of the spectrum.

These gifts have been made in various ways. In some cases, frequencies were allocated to what were judged to be deserving causes, like the emergency services – or the forestry department, which received allocations even in parts of the country where there were no forests. In other cases, they were allocated to the radio stations that had first made use of them – a regularisation of squatters 'rights known as 'grandfathering'. In yet other cases, where there were competing commercial interests, the Commission selected the user that they judged would make best use of the spectrum following a sort of 'beauty contest'. At best, these gifts lack transparency and discriminate against new entrants to the market. At worst they are inefficient, in that some frequencies are overcrowded and others under-used; unfair, in that the allocation is subject to lobbying; and open to corruption.

Ronald Coase (1959:25) made the case that radio spectrum could be allocated most efficiently by establishing private property rights in the spectrum and then auctioning these rights to the highest bidders. Nearly half a century later, when it became obvious that there was a need to allocate additional spectrum to mobile phone companies so that they could provide data-rich third generation (3G) services such as video calling and Internet access, many governments decided to follow his recommendation. In April 2000 five companies paid a total of over £22 billion to the Radiocommunications Agency, acting on behalf of the British government, for licences that gave them exclusive use of this natural resource for 20 years. This generated far more revenue than any privatisation and, at an annual rate of £1.1 billion, provides nearly 0.4 per cent of the government's revenue from all forms of taxation.

Similar auctions of spectrum across Europe provided governments with US$ 100 billion in a way that drew little protest from the general public – certainly nothing like the reaction they would have faced if they had increased Income Tax, VAT or Fuel Duty. Perhaps this was just because it didn't seem to challenge the self-interest of many people. I prefer to think that it was because people understood the government's stated objective for the auctions: to utilise the available spectrum with optimum efficiency, promote effective and sustainable competition, and design an auction which was best judged to realise the full economic value of the spectrum to consumers, industry and the taxpayer (Barbara Roche 1998).

What sort of property rights have the telecoms operators acquired? The arrangement is a 20-year lease, not ownership in the sense of a freehold or a right to use the spectrum forever. This should ensure that this natural resource benefits us all for all time, unless the government succumbs to lobbying to extend the lease.

The essential feature of an auction is that the successful bidder offers what is, in their judgement, the full value of the right to use the spectrum for the 20 years. It establishes the market rent of the spectrum, its resource rent.

The auction was possible because the electromagnetic spectrum was not already in private ownership. It is relatively straightforward to treat the environment in this way when there are no pre-existing private property claims on it, particularly where it is recognised to be the property of the state.

There have been a variety of criticisms of the way the spectrum auctions were handled, but the great advantage of an auction is that it allocates the spectrum to the highest bidders and so:

o   is fair and transparent

o   ensures that the spectrum is put to the best use by allocating it efficiently – to whoever can make the fullest use of it, as reflected by the profits they expect to make

o   promotes competition – in particular, by not putting new entrants at a disadvantage.

This is only a start: the 3G bandwidth is a tiny proportion of the whole electromagnetic spectrum, which is itself only one aspect of the environment. But it is a start. The alternative would have been for the state to give this valuable resource to its favoured telecoms providers.

What use should be made of the revenue from the auctions? In a microcosm, who should benefit from the wealth of the natural world? You might think that the state should be acting on behalf of telephone users, and that the telecoms companies should receive the revenue and use it either to reduce their charges to customers or reward their shareholders (James MacDonald 2000:6). Or you might think that the state should be acting on behalf of the whole population and see the revenue as compensation to all of us for the operators 'monopoly rights to something that has been provided by nature and to which the rest of us abdicate our possible claims – the stewardship approach.

The spectrum auction provides an illustration of how, in an ideal stewardship world, all aspects of the natural world would be allocated. The natural world would be held in trust; users would pay an annual fee or charge; and the revenue would be distributed equally amongst the whole population, compensating everybody who is excluded from using it for their own purposes.

So, stewardship has, in the small but significant arena of allocating the electromagnetic spectrum, already been partially implemented in the UK – though not by name.

Climate change

The principles of stewardship have also received considerable support as an approach to tackling climate change.

The first steps towards the behaviour change required to tackle climate change are for us to recognise that there is a problem and to decide to do something about it. The final steps require action – at individual, organisational, national and global levels. Between recognition and action there are several possible collective actions to support the necessary behaviour change – including regulation, taxation, legislation and private property rights. Property rights are simple and transparent to implement.

One property rights approach is known as 'cap and trade'. The first step here is for a body to take responsibility for managing the atmosphere, just as national governments took responsibility for managing the radio spectrum. Ideally this would be a global body to tackle what is a global problem, but each country could take responsibility for managing its own share.

The next step is for this body, or an independent regulator, to decide the current maximum permissible rate of emissions. This 'cap' is divided into emissions permits of manageable size, and these permits are a form of property right. Any organisation that introduces carbon into the economy (by mining coal, drilling oil, deforestation and so on), or the equivalent for other greenhouse gases, has to surrender the appropriate number of permits. Anybody holding emissions permits can sell them – the permits are tradable, which is why the whole edifice is known as cap and trade. That much is fairly uncontroversial, but for this approach to work the cap must be set at an appropriate level and the surrender of permits and prohibition of emissions in excess of surrendered permits must be enforced.

The way that we allocate these property rights will have a profound effect on the course of the next century. One option is to follow the example of William the Conqueror, who allocated the land of England to his supporters, and allocate ownership of permits to release greenhouse gases at a certain rate in perpetuity to those industries that are already doing so.

Peter Barnes (2001:12 asks the question 'Who owns the sky?' and suggests that the answer should be 'all of us'. He proposes that the atmosphere be held in trust for everybody by a non-governmental Sky Trust. The Trust would auction to corporations the emissions permits that they would need to surrender when introducing carbon into the economy. Each permit would entitle the holder to introduce a defined amount of carbon in a given period of time. Its price would be determined by the auction – it would be a market price.

Allocating ownership by grandfathering enriches the polluting corporations with a one-off gift, while the Sky Trust auctions would enrich all of us for ever by paying an equal Environmental Dividend to each person. There is a growing consensus that an approach like the Sky Trust offers the fairest and most effective way to tackle the problem of climate change.

The proposed Sky Trust is exactly the sort of Environment Stewardship Trust that would be found in a stewardship economy (Chapter 7) In the later chapters of his book, Peter Barnes suggests that in his ideal future many Trusts would come into being to manage different aspects of what he calls 'the New Commons – ' natural assets like biodiversity and quietude, and societal assets like democracy (2001:105). Each Trust would contribute to a consolidated dividend that everybody would receive.

Although there are some differences from the proposals in this book, and he does not explicitly propose charges for the use of land as well as other parts of the environment, Peter Barnes is describing what I would recognise as features of a stewardship economy.

Summary: There are remarkable similarities between possible approaches to the allocation of rural land in a low-consumption economy, radio spectrum in a high-consumption economy and greenhouse gas emissions on a global scale. In each case, the fairest and most efficient way to allocate the use of the natural world seems to be to hold it in trust, rent it to the highest bidder and distribute the revenue to everybody. This is the essence of stewardship.

PART II STEWARDSHIP IN ESSENCE

Chapter 4 summarises the purpose, principles and practice of stewardship and sets out its advantages over ownership.

Chapter 5 sets out a few key points in the history of the ideas.

Chapter 4   Purpose, principles and practice

This chapter describes the purpose, principles and practice of stewardship – first as they apply to plots of land and then to the environment. It sets out the main advantages that stewardship has over ownership. The chapter describes a mature steady-state stewardship economy – the question of whether and how we might get there from an ownership economy is left until Part V.

Purpose

The purpose of stewardship is to ensure the efficient and sustainable use of the natural world; and to provide social justice by ensuring that everybody benefits, equally and fairly, from the wealth of the natural world.

Principles

The two underlying principles of stewardship are that:

We are stewards, not owners, of the natural world

The steward of a part of the natural world has:

- o *the right of access* – to use it in the way that they choose, within the constraints of any relevant regulations
- o *the responsibility of care* – to manage it responsibly and husband it for future generations, accepting liability for any damage done to it
- o *the duty of compensation* – to pay an annual fee, equal to its market rent, into a fund that is used to benefit everyone
- o *ownership*, in the conventional sense, of any buildings or other improvements.

Everybody benefits equally

Everybody is entitled to an equal share of the wealth of the natural world and receives a guaranteed income – a 'common treasury for all mankind.' (Gerard Winstanley 1649:9) – in the form of both a Universal Income from stewardship fees and an Environmental Dividend.

Practice

Stewardship of land

The land is held in trust

In a stewardship economy, a Land Stewardship Trust holds all land in trust for its people. This Trust grants secure tenure of plots of land to stewards who pay an annual charge – the stewardship fee. It is a national body, because it is the state that protects territorial integrity and guarantees security of tenure to the steward, but it is administered locally.

Every plot of land has a steward

A person or other legal entity is responsible for acting as the steward for each plot of land.

Stewardship is a form of private property

Property systems are classified according to who has the power to determine how the property is used. Four sorts of agent have been recognised since the development of Roman law and each is associated with a different property system – private property, collective (public) property, common property and open access regimes.

Decisions about the use of land in a stewardship economy (including decisions about excluding others from its use) are made by the steward and not, for example, by the collective. Stewardship is therefore a form of private property.

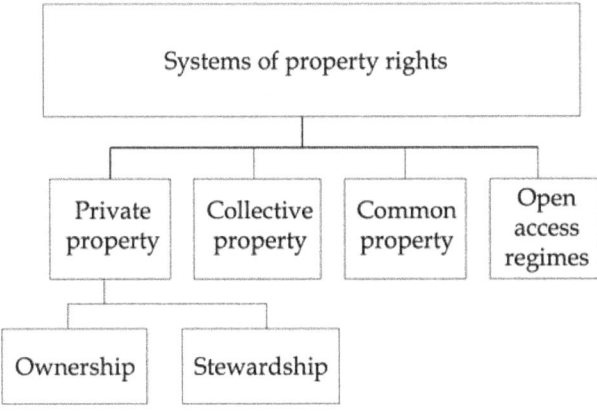

Stewards own their buildings and other improvements

Stewardship is a form of property that is appropriate for the natural world. Ownership remains appropriate, in a stewardship economy, for things that are produced by human effort and ingenuity (artefacts). This includes buildings and other improvements, even where these cannot be physically separated from the land.

Stewardship fee equal to the market rent

Each steward pays a stewardship fee that is equal to the market rent of the land.

Stewardship is determined at auction

In the new land market, a steward who wants to dispose of a plot of land, or an interest in a plot such as a leasehold, informs the Land Stewardship Trust. The Trust conducts an auction at which the plot or interest is allocated to the person who bids the highest annual stewardship fee – its market rent. This incoming steward also acquires the liability to pay to the outgoing steward the value of the buildings and other improvements to the land.

In this way the Land Stewardship Trust collects the *whole* of the market rent – not through a desire to raise revenue for the state, but because an auction provides a fair and efficient way of allocating access to land.

Some of the revenue takes the place of taxes

In a stewardship economy, some of the revenue from stewardship fees is used to finance government expenditure. This reduces the need for conventional taxes such as those on income, enterprise or value added. This, in turn, reduces the deadweight loss of taxation and so provides a stimulus to the economy.

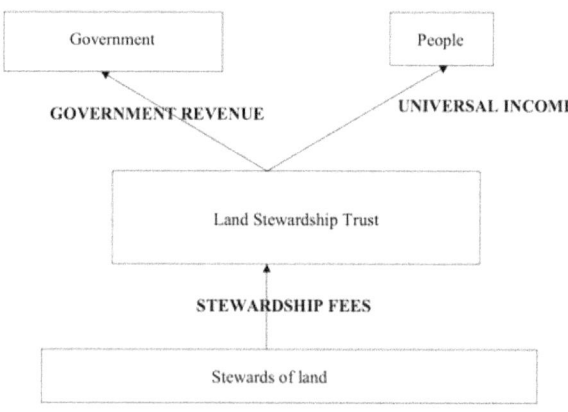

The rest is distributed as a Universal Income

The rest of the revenue is distributed to everybody, unconditionally, as a Universal Income. This is compensation for allowing stewards the exclusive right to occupy and use their land.

People contribute in proportion to the land they use

People contribute to financing both government spending and the Universal Income in proportion to the value of the land they occupy and use. People who have more than their equal share of land are net contributors, while people who have less than their equal share are net recipients.

Stewards are responsible for looking after their site

Each steward is responsible for damage (disimprovement) to their site.

The market value (purchase price) of land is zero

The market value (purchase price) of an asset, such as land, reflects the stream of revenue, net of all expenses, that it is expected to generate in the future. The market rent of any plot of land, minus the stewardship fee that has to be paid for it, is zero. So, the market value of land in an established stewardship economy is zero, too.

Stewardship of the environment

The environment is held in trust

Just as with the land, aspects of the environment (for example the atmosphere, oceans, fisheries, mineral deposits and the radio spectrum) are held by Environment Stewardship Trusts, which manage the resource for which they are responsible. The Trusts may use regulation, subsidies and taxes but are most likely to make use of private property rights in the form of charges for permits that allow a certain amount of use for a defined period of time (Chapter 7) and are surrendered when the permit-holder uses the environment.

Permits are auctioned

The number of permits is decided in consultation with the regulatory body for that aspect of the environment.

Each permit is allocated by auction – as in the case of the spectrum auctions. Permits are a property right to use some aspect of the environment for a defined length of time, for example a year, and the auctions establish the price (resource rent) for that use of the environment. In this way individuals and organisations that make use of the environment pay a charge for doing so.

This provides a practical way to allocate the environment to those who most want to use it (or at least to those who are prepared to pay most to use it).

Permits are tradable

The permits are tradable. This enables their price, both on a day-to-day basis and at any date in the future, to be established by the market.

Renewable resources – the Environmental Dividend

The revenue from the auction of the permits for the use of renewable resources is not available as government revenue. It is divided into equal shares and paid to each individual as an Environmental Dividend.

In this way those who use more than an equal share of renewable resources make net payments to those who use less than an equal share.

Non-renewable resources – investing resource rents

If we are going to deplete non-renewable resources and still live sustainably, we need to invest the revenue from these resources in forms of capital that will benefit future generations – particularly in substitutes for the resource in question. This means that revenue from non-renewable resources is not distributed as an Environmental Dividend.

For pragmatic reasons it may be necessary to relax the sustainability requirement for some non-renewable resources and distribute the revenue as an Environmental Dividend as if the resource were renewable (Chapter 7).

True cost prices

When an oil company or a fisherman has to purchase an extraction permit, they experience the cost of using the environment (which economists refer to as a resource rent) in the costs of their business. They have to pass this cost on to whoever buys their oil or fish. Consumers pay a price that reflects the true cost of goods or services, including both the usual costs to the firm and these resource rents – a price that economists refer to as the social cost. Choices about what to consume are then guided by the true costs of goods and services, so environmental costs are taken into account and externalities minimised.

Advantages

Stewardship
   o   is a form of private property that allocates land and natural resources more fairly (Chapter 12) and more efficiently (Chapters 6 & 7) than ownership.

Stewardship fees
   o   are fairer and more efficient than any form of taxation (including other sorts of land tax) (Chapter 12)
   o   ensure that if a community does something that increases the market rent of land – such as improving its transport connections, or making it a safer place to live – it is the whole community, not just the owner of that land, who benefits (Chapter 12)
   o   impose no deadweight loss on the economy (unlike Income Tax, Corporation Tax, VAT, Council Tax, Stamp Duty Land Tax and other taxes) (Chapters 8 & 12)
   o   discourage what we want to discourage (under-use and inefficient use of land, derelict sites and urban sprawl (Chapter 6), which increase the fuel and time costs of commuting); not what we want to encourage (work, enterprise and construction) (Chapter 8)
   o   stabilise house prices and prevent house price bubbles from developing and bursting (Chapter 8)

- enable transport infrastructure to become self-financing (Chapter 10)
- transfer wealth (in conjunction with the Universal Income) from prosperous areas to poorer ones (Chapter 6)
- are cheap to collect and simple to administer (Chapter 12)
- are difficult to avoid or evade (Chapter 12).

Universal Income
- guarantees an income for all as a right (Chapter 9)
- supports people during all forms of work, study and training (Chapter 9)
- removes or reduces the indignity and poor take-up of means-tested benefits (Chapters 9)
- reduces inequalities (Chapter 9)
- encourages saving and self-reliance (Chapter 12)
- is cheap and simple to administer (Chapter 12)
- is difficult to defraud (Chapter 12).

Environmental charges
- reduce environmental damage by ensuring that the prices consumers pay reflect true costs (Chapters 7 & 12).

The Environmental Dividend
- compensates those who use less than their fair share of renewable resources (Chapter 7 & 12).

Stewardship economy
- is fairer, more effective and more efficient (Chapter 12) than an ownership economy.

In summary: Stewardship rests on the distinction between the natural world and artefacts. It challenges the assumption that the natural world can be owned in the same way that things can be.

A stewardship economy is rooted in personal liberty and private property. For all artefacts (such as personal possessions, machinery and buildings) property rights take the conventional form of 'ownership'. But for land and the environment, property rights in a stewardship economy are different. The steward of land has the right to occupy and use the land as well as the responsibility to ensure it is looked after, taking formal responsibility for damage done. Most importantly, the market rent of land is not the property of its steward but is shared amongst the whole community.

Stewardship can be seen as a proposal to reform the tax-benefit system – a new look at the way we share the benefits and responsibilities of living together in society. From another perspective, it can be seen as a re-evaluation of the relationship between people and the Earth. It represents a change in the ethical basis of private property as radical as that which occurred when the acceptance that human beings could not be owned led to the abolition of slavery.

Remember, though, that this description is of the ideal – an established, mature, steady-state stewardship economy. It is only worth considering whether it would be possible to make a transition to stewardship from an established ownership economy (Chapter 14) if a stewardship economy is attractive (Part III), fundamentally fair and efficient (Chapter 12) and a practical proposition (Chapter 13)

Chapter 5   History

Stewardship is not a new idea, but an old idea whose time has come. It brings together several traditions and combines these with the possibilities offered by information technology.

You may be familiar with the term 'Land Value Taxation' and wonder why I use 'stewardship' to refer to a charge equal to 100 per cent of market rent; and why I use the term 'land' with its everyday meaning, not the one it usually carries in economics. If so, you may want to go to the Glossary which explains the reasons as well as providing definitions for key terms including land, environment, natural world, rent, market rent, stewardship, stewardship fee, stewardship economy and Universal Income; and a link to the full web-based glossary.

The underlying principle of stewardship – that the natural world should be held as private property but that everybody is entitled to an equal share of its wealth – can be traced back at least as far as Thomas Spence's *A lecture read to the philosophical society in Newcastle* (1775a).

For the last quarter of a century, its elements – Land Value Taxation, environmental pricing and Citizen's Income – have been on the agenda of the Green movement as part of a strategy for achieving a peaceful, equitable and sustainable future. James Robertson has championed the interdependence between these elements in a series of books, particularly in his publication for the New Economics Foundation *Benefits and Taxes* (1994).

Rents as common property

Thomas Spence

There is a long tradition of calls for land to be held as common property, most notably in England by Gerrard Winstanley and the Diggers. Thomas Spence's distinctive contribution was to advocate the continuation of private tenure of land, while at the same time the parish would collect rent for its use and use the revenue as common property (1775a).

Thomas Paine

Thomas Paine asserted that every individual is born with a legitimate claim on the Earth. This was not a proposal to return to a state of common or collective property, but to adopt a form of private property in which the proprietor of land owes to the community a 'ground rent' (Thomas Paine 1797a:4). This would, however, be collected 'at the moment that property is passing by the death of one person to the possession of another'.

Hillel Steiner

Hillel Steiner is a political philosopher whose influential *An essay on rights* develops an approach that has come to be known as left-libertarianism, which locates justice in a set of rights to self and to external property.

Like right-libertarians he asserts a person's self-ownership and their right to own artefacts. While they can acquire title to these as a result of production, voluntary transfer and redress (1994:266), they have a right to appropriate no more than an equal portion of unowned things like the natural world.

He therefore argues that, in a fully appropriated world, the possession of a just title to initially unowned things obliges the possessor to pay every person an equal share of their value (1994:271). This obligation is global not national in extent.

Land Value Taxation

Henry George

The most influential campaigner for the collection of a charge on the market rent of land was the land rights philosopher and political economist, Henry George. The inspiration for his best-known work, *Progress and Poverty* (1879), was his experience as editor of a San Francisco newspaper that the main beneficiaries of the arrival of the railroad on the west coast were not entrepreneurs or working people but landowners.

Two of his most important proposals are key features of stewardship. He advocated collecting close to 100 per cent of the market rent of land as a Land Value Tax. And he advocated removing all other forms of taxation, with their negative effects on people and the economy, so that a Land Value Tax would be a single tax (1879 Book VIII Chapter II : 365).

100 per cent of market rent

It is not possible to point to examples where 100 per cent of the market rent of land has been collected as tax, but smaller proportions of the market rent have been collected in many jurisdictions. This is what most people who describe themselves as supporters of Land Value Taxation or 'Georgists' now advocate, for very understandable pragmatic reasons. Stewardship, which in its mature form requires a stewardship fee of 100 per cent of the market rent, is very much at the radical end of the spectrum of proposals to collect charges on land values.

Universal Income

Thomas Paine proposed that a fund be established, drawing on the ground rent, and that payments from the fund be made unconditionally to rich and poor alike. He suggested that it should provide a pension for older people and a lump sum payment at the age of twenty-one – an interesting combination of a Universal

Income with a Universal Capital Grant – with additional payments to blind and lame people.

The idea of an unconditional income resurfaced several times in the twentieth century (Hermione Parker 1989:121) and is usually referred to as 'Basic Income' or 'Citizen's Income'. In the 1920s Clifford Hugh Douglas (1924:204) suggested that the workings of the business system are impaired by a lack of aggregate demand and proposed that the state should distribute new money as a birthright to every citizen, whether in employment or not, in the form of a dividend called 'Social Credit'. Juliet Rhys Williams in 1943 argued against the Beveridge plan and advocated that the state should pay an income to every man, woman and child to ensure that they have the necessities for a healthy life, though this was to be conditional on the person signing a social contract. This proposal, stripped of conditionality, was further developed by James Meade and Brandon Rhys Williams, and continues to attract significant support.

In summary: Thomas Paine described the system of landed property as having 'stolen imperceptibly upon the world' (1797a:6). Stewardship challenges this system. In Part III I describe what economies and societies could look like when we abandon the idea that the Earth is an object that can be owned in the same way as an artefact. *Stewardship Economy: Private property without private ownership* embraces the understanding that we are stewards of the Earth with responsibilities to everybody currently alive, to future generations and to the Earth itself

PART III STEWARDSHIP IN PRACTICE

'It's not a bad world – just badly organised '(Robb Johnson)

There are many ways in which a stewardship economy differs from an ownership economy. These include the way that land is used; the provision of housing; the development of regions and cities; the management of the environment; the whole way that the economy functions; the way that the tax-benefit system is organised; the distribution of wealth; the funding of transport and utilities and the functioning of the global economy.

Part III briefly outlines these differences. It provides an overview of the wide range of interlocking impacts of stewardship. Each section is a summary of material that is presented at greater depth in other books in the series which contain explanations, evidence and references.

The consequences of implementing stewardship can be anticipated but not predicted, so *Stewardship Economy: Private property without private ownership* provides a sketch of the main features of a stewardship economy rather than a detailed blueprint for a new society.

Remember that this description of a stewardship economy is of a steady state – transition from an ownership economy is described in Chapter 14.

Throughout Part III, each section is presented across two facing pages. The left hand page describes the situation as it is in an ownership economy. The right hand page describes it as it could be in an established stewardship economy.

Chapter 6 Land

Land use

In an ownership economy....

Over-investment in land. One of the reasons that people buy land is because they expect it to increase in value - there is often a speculative tinge to land purchase.

Under-use of land. There are tens of thousands of hectares of derelict and underused land in the UK as well as large numbers of sites that could be better used.

People generally attribute under-use to delays in the planning system. This is a real problem, and in any economy planning needs to be resourced to operate quickly but with rigour and democratic accountability.

Planning is not, however, the only cause of under-use – parcels of land may need to be assembled for development, and it may take time to rehabilitate degraded land.

The most significant reason for the under-use of land, however, is that there is remarkably little economic incentive to use it. If the owner of capital goods or money does not put them to use their value falls – machinery rusts and becomes obsolete, money under the mattress devalues with inflation. If a worker withdraws their labour, they lose their income. But when people expect that land values will rise over time, it can make good economic sense not to sell underused land but to hold on to it and profit by the increase in its value. Developers may build up land banks that are kept idle for decades, land is often bought for investment or speculation not for use and supermarkets have been accused of buying sites to prevent their rivals from setting up in competition.

This underuse of land is exacerbated by the system of local taxes – Council Tax and the Non-Domestic (Business) Rates may be reduced when buildings are empty.

In a stewardship economy....

A steward owns buildings, or other improvements, in the conventional way and can lease or hire them out.

Availability of land. A steward of unimproved land (with no buildings on it) cannot profit by renting it out, as they have to pay a stewardship fee equal to the market rent. They can anticipate no capital gain. Stewards have a financial incentive either to develop or to dispose of undeveloped land unless they soon plan to put it to use themselves.

There is no need to borrow a capital sum to access land. Stewardship increases the amount of land supplied on the market, which lowers its market rent. Land (with or without buildings) is more readily available in a stewardship economy, whether for housing, business or agriculture.

Land use. The incentive to put land to use in a stewardship economy stimulates regeneration and discourages the dereliction of sites and buildings that is not just an eyesore but promotes vandalism and crime. Any site that is relatively underused is under pressure to develop, so all land in a local area with the same planning restrictions tends to be developed to the same extent.

Stewardship leads to urban design that is more compact with fewer empty or unused sites, less urban sprawl and shorter commuting distances. It can even provide an automatic market-based subsidy for the rehabilitation of contaminated or degraded land if the Land Stewardship Trust accepts bids for a negative stewardship fee (subsidy) where there are no positive bids.

Removal of speculation. The cost of land is constant. There is no speculation. There is an incentive to maintain and develop buildings throughout the business cycle.

Planning

In an ownership economy....

Need for planning restrictions. In ownership economies most landowners, most of the time, put their land to good use. But their idea of a good use may not coincide with the wishes of the rest of society. This is why we need a planning system that can put restrictions on what can be built, and where.

Planning is important but imperfect. There have been plenty of examples of unnecessary delays; planning principles that seem, in retrospect, ill-advised; and even corruption. One current issue is the difficulty of getting planning permission for low-cost, energy-efficient, low-impact rural homes. But the planning system needs support and improvement, not weakening.

Planning needs to be open, transparent, democratically accountable and free from corruption.

The financial cost of planning restrictions. Planning restrictions affect not just the use of land but its value. In the South East of England, land restricted to agricultural use can rise in value a thousand-fold if planning permission is granted for residential development; providing the owner with a massive windfall gain as a result of the planning decisions of the whole society. Conversely if planning restrictions are imposed the owner of the site bears the cost as the property falls in value, even though the restrictions are imposed for the benefit of society as a whole.

Permissive planning. One problem for planners is that when a planning authority grants permission for development of a site, there is no guarantee that this will go ahead. The owner may be content just to see the value of their land rise without having to carry out any development. Planning in an ownership economy is permissive not prescriptive.

In a stewardship economy....

Each steward is under pressure to put their site to its best use. Might activities of low economic but high social value – such as affordable housing, businesses on the edge of profitability, allotments, smallholdings and amenity areas – be squeezed out and their land overdeveloped?

While this pressure is real, there is a counterbalance. The pressure to make best use of *all* sites releases land onto the market. This reduces, but does not remove, the pressure on sites that are less developed but of high social value.

Need for planning restrictions. The need to prevent over-development means that a fair, transparent and effective planning system is even more necessary in a stewardship economy than in an ownership economy. It is placed under intense scrutiny because the market rent of each plot of land, and so its stewardship fee, depends on the planning restrictions that are placed on that plot. The planning system therefore lies at the heart of a stewardship economy.

There are several ways in which planning has a different impact in a stewardship economy:

The financial benefit of planning restrictions. When planning restrictions are imposed on a plot of land, the steward is compensated by a fall in its stewardship fee. There are no windfall gains to be had from removing planning restrictions. Many planning applications from stewards will, therefore, be to *restrict* the use of their land.

"Prescriptive" planning. Planning decisions are much more likely to be put into effect. Once planning permission is in place the steward has to pay higher stewardship fees even if they do not carry out the development for which permission has been granted. This means that they are likely to develop the land (or transfer it to somebody who will) so that it generates the necessary income.

Regions and cities

In an ownership economy....

Geographical inequalities. In ownership economies some regions are prosperous and have high levels of income, employment and land values. Other regions are relatively deprived with poverty, unemployment and poor health; and here land prices are lower. Younger people and those who are more highly trained, who can imagine finding a better life elsewhere, leave the area. A downward spiral often takes hold in which enterprise is discouraged from locating in the area, or even from staying there, by the lack of skilled workers and poor infrastructure.

Prosperous areas have problems, too. Land, and so housing, is expensive and it is difficult for essential workers to be able to afford to live there.

Regeneration. Governments, and free-trade areas like the European Union, recognise that unequal development between regions is a price to be paid for a trading economy in which there is mobility of capital and labour. They attempt to counteract its worst consequences by making transfer payments from prosperous to deprived regions, often in the form of regeneration programmes that focus on replacing buildings and infrastructure and stimulating enterprise and employment. These transfers require political and administrative input, are intermittent, unpredictable and potentially corrupt – but essential in an ownership economy.

Cities. Geographical differences also develop within cities, with areas of deprivation often located on just 'the other side of the tracks' from prosperous localities. Deprivation has negative impacts, such as crime and the fear of crime; but the availability of low-value land close to areas of prosperity also enables cities to be dynamic and diverse places in which start-up businesses and artists can establish themselves in localities that have fallen out of fashion and out of use.

In a stewardship economy….

Greater geographical equality. The combination of stewardship fees with Universal Income automatically redistributes wealth from prosperous locations (with high per capita land values) to deprived locations (with low per capita land values), thereby reducing inequalities between individuals, neighbourhoods and regions. Mobile private sector firms have an incentive to re-locate and invest capital in more deprived areas where stewardship fees, and so business costs, are low.

Regeneration. Transfers of Universal Income serve the same general purpose in a stewardship economy as regeneration programmes do in an ownership economy. They support deprived regions and localities, though the beneficiaries are individuals rather than infrastructure projects. This has the advantage of avoiding the layers of politics and administration with all their costs but the disadvantage that increased individual wealth will not provide street lighting, public transport and other public goods. Stewardship does, however, provide alternative ways of funding infrastructure.

The Universal Income makes it worth people's while to accept lower-paid or part-time jobs, thereby stimulating the local economy.

Cities. Income inequalities are reduced, and health and wellbeing improve while crime and disrespect fall. Diversity is maintained by the planning system.

Development becomes both uniform, with fewer areas of dereliction and underinvestment; and so more compact, with a reduction in commuting times. Transport becomes self-funding.

Housing

In an ownership economy....

Financial advantages of ownership. Owning one's own home generally provides more security, independence and financial gain than renting.

At the time of purchase the monthly cost of buying a home is, usually, broadly comparable with that of renting. As time goes on the cost of renting rises, as the property's value rises; while a homeowner's costs are broadly constant until the mortgage is paid off, when they fall to zero.

Another financial advantage for the homeowner is that the market value of the property tends to increase in real terms across an economic cycle. This is amplified by the tax system, which exempts homes from Capital Gains Tax.

However, some of the apparent financial benefits of owner-occupation are less than might appear at first sight. The increasing value of a home can only be realised by giving up home ownership and becoming a tenant, or by downsizing. And houses may fall in value, threatening some owners with negative equity, either during an economic downturn or when local developments reduce land values.

Availability of homes. The usual response to the lack of affordable homes is to advocate more home-building and relaxation of planning restrictions. But there are already hundreds of thousands of empty homes, and in some parts of the country it is the demand for second homes that prices local people out of the market and destroys communities.

Key workers. Many essential public service workers find it is impossible to buy a home in the area in which they work. There have been imaginative responses, such as Community Land Trusts in which land is held in common while buildings are owned by their occupiers; but the state has generally had to provide ongoing subsidies for rented and shared-ownership homes.

In a stewardship economy....

House prices do not rise unless the building is extended, but they do not fall either unless the building deteriorates.

Cost of housing. A steward in a stewardship economy pays a charge for the land they use that is equal to its market rent, just like a tenant in an ownership economy. But the steward owns the building, while the tenant leases it.

The financial position of a steward is apparently not as advantageous as that of an owner-occupier in an ownership economy – both because there are no capital gains and because stewardship fees rise over the course of time to reflect the rising market rent of land. But stewards receive Universal Income, which counteracts these higher costs for those living on sites of less than average per capita value.

In a stewardship economy, therefore, people feel free to rent as there is no financial pressure to get on the housing ladder. There is less need to go into debt to buy a home. Landlords do not profit (after paying stewardship fees) from renting out land, or from rising land prices, and earn their income in the same way that a car lease company earns its – by providing and maintaining an asset, in this case buildings.

Availability of homes. There are more homes available as there is financial pressure to put empty homes and derelict land to use; and there are fewer second homes, as there is no financial incentive to invest in them.

Key workers. Housing costs may be too high for low-paid workers to live close to their work, even when stewardship has been fully implemented. One solution, for public service workers, is for their pay routinely to include an element that reflects local stewardship fees. Another is to use the planning system to restrict some properties to low-paid workers, which lowers their market rent as the pool of permissible willing buyers is smaller and less wealthy.

Chapter 7   Environment

Environment and land

In an ownership economy....

I distinguish between land (the solid surface of the planet) and the environment (amenities, resources and sinks). The environment includes spaces on the surface like rivers, lakes and oceans; above the surface like the atmosphere and electromagnetic spectrum; or below the surface. There are several reasons for making the distinction between land and the environment:

Creation of new property rights. One is that, while the property rights to most areas of land are well established, it is only now that property rights to the environment are being allocated. Many of these, such as the right to pollute, are being gifted to organisations that have squatted on this property and that governments are reluctant to disturb. Some property rights to the environment, such as a lease on the spectrum for mobile phones, have however been allocated by auction; and the UK government favours the auction of carbon permits and aircraft landing slots.

True cost prices. Another reason for distinguishing between land and the environment is that, while most land is put to its best use when a single person or organisation determines how it is used, most aspects of the environment appropriately have multiple users. There is often a maximum acceptable level of use – a certain number of walkers per day on a wilderness trail, a certain amount of water that can be abstracted from a river each year. When ownership economies have tried to limit environmental use to these levels, they have had the choice of using regulation or the price mechanism to shape choices. The state may influence prices either by imposing a tax (as it does on petrol) or by selling permits to use the environment (as it did with the spectrum auctions).

In a stewardship economy....

Environment Stewardship Trusts. Where there is competition for the use of a particular aspect of the environment, for example a river system or the atmospheric sink for carbon dioxide, an Environment Stewardship Trust is established – for example a Watershed Stewardship Trust.

This Trust holds that aspect of the environment in trust and is responsible for ensuring that the users of the environment make the best sustainable use of it. It may do so by making and enforcing regulations, like fishing seasons; or it may auction tradable permits to use the environment.

The Trust may be a state agency; an independent not-for-profit body; or a corporation trading for profit and operating under a franchise that is time-limited and awarded from time to time to the highest qualified bidder.

The Trust is subject to the rulings of a regulator, an independent body that reviews the evidence and sets criteria for environmental protection that the Trust must meet – perhaps including the maximum number of permits to be issued in each time period.

Tradable permits. The property rights that an environmental permit confers are transferable, and their price is established in secondary and futures markets.

True cost prices. Auctioning the appropriate number of tradable permits ensures that any firm or individual that makes use of the environment pays the true cost of doing so. This means that the firm has to charge a higher price for its services or products than it would in an ownership economy. This true cost price includes the cost to the environment and to society as well as the production cost and is intended to reduce consumption, and so to ensure that economic activity is sustainable.

Amenities and resources

In an ownership economy....

Amenities. An amenity is a place that that is enjoyed directly – for example recreation space – rather than being transformed through the process of production. It could often be used more profitably for another purpose, such as housing. The pressure to develop amenities can only be resisted by an altruistic owner or by the planning system.

While neighbouring properties benefit from a nearby amenity they do not have to pay for the privilege, so the costs of maintenance fall entirely on the owner of the amenity. And this owner may have understandable reasons for denying access to others as this deprives the owner of privacy, imposes costs and may reduce the property's value.

Renewable resources. Most renewable resources – for example water, air, electromagnetic spectrum – have in the past been freely available (open access regimes). This means that firms have not faced the true cost of using these resources. This in turn has meant that the price of their products does not reflect their true cost, more of the products are consumed and more of the resource is used than is sustainable. Governments have attempted to reduce the use of renewable resources to sustainable levels by regulation, through the price mechanism or by subsidising alternatives.

Non-renewable resources. There are few limits on the extraction of non-renewable resources, other than those of the cost of extraction and local planning restrictions. The costs of resource depletion have been borne by the environment not by the firm (externalised), and resources may have been depleted more rapidly than is wise. Environmental economists have demonstrated that consumption can be maintained at the highest sustainable level if the revenue (resource rent) obtained from resource extraction is invested in alternative forms of capital, including alternatives to the resource in question.

In a stewardship economy....

Amenities. The planning system sets limits on the development of amenity sites, and so on their stewardship fees; and there are other ways in which stewardship improves access to amenities or supports them financially.

When people have a right of access over land this reduces the market rent of the property, and so reduces the fees the steward pays; and in this way the whole population compensates the steward for the right of access.

When neighbouring sites benefit from a nearby amenity their stewardship fees are higher, and it is possible for the Land Stewardship Trust to reserve (hypothecate) that part of the stewardship fees for the upkeep of the amenity.

Renewable resources. In a stewardship economy the relevant Environment Stewardship Trust establishes, in conjunction with its regulator, the maximum sustainable rate of extraction. Each year it auctions permits for this amount.

The revenue is distributed equally as an Environmental Dividend to everybody in the country, or internationally if there is agreement to do so.

Non-renewable resources. The extraction of a non-renewable resource may be restricted both by the requirement for extraction permits at a national level and by local planning restrictions on the site in question.

The revenue is invested for the benefit of future generations, particularly in the development of alternatives to the non-renewable resource in question.

The impact of true cost pricing on firms. Each firm is able to pass on the average level of environmental cost to their consumers in a true cost price for their goods and services, so the only businesses that are penalised financially are those that cause greater environmental damage than the average for their industry.

Pollution

In an ownership economy....

Pollution may have its main impact at the site where it is released, on sites that neighbour it, or more widely. The release of pollutants is powerfully influenced by the system of property rights for land and the environment.

Damage to a single site. There is least restraint where property is held as an open access regime (e.g., dumping of waste at sea) or as collective property (e.g., heavy metal pollution from state-owned industries in Eastern Europe). Pollution may also be difficult to limit where property is managed as common property if the governance institutions are not strong enough.

Pollution may be reduced in ownership economies by transferring open access regimes and collective property into private ownership. But even in private ownership, the financial incentives to avoid polluting one's own land are not as strong as might be expected. The cost of owning land is not experienced as current expenditure but as sunk costs. If land value is reduced by pollution, the owner experiences no cost in the current business accounts. And the value of the land tends anyway to rise over the course of time, disguising any loss in value due to pollution. Regulation is necessary.

Impact on neighbouring sites. Pollution may be exported, by contamination of air or water, to neighbouring sites. This problem has been tackled in ownership economies either by regulation or by legislation that allows the owner of affected properties to obtain compensation from the polluter.

Discounting. In our economic decisions we do not value the future as much as the present – we discount the future, often (perhaps surprisingly) by something like the nominal rate of interest. Greens take the long-term future very seriously and differ from other political groups in setting a low or zero discount rate for policy decisions.

In a stewardship economy....

Stewardship offers a different approach to pollution control by providing a different system of property rights. A steward is responsible for protecting their land from pollution and neglect.

Damage to a single site. The cost of any damage (disimprovement) is assessed (when a site is sold, or annually if it is known to be at risk) and the steward has to pay this amount to the Land Stewardship Trust. This discourages a firm from polluting its own site.

Impact on neighbouring sites. Stewardship provides a straightforward universal mechanism for preventing people from shifting (externalising) the costs of pollution onto their neighbours. When a site suffers damage the steward has the duty to inform the Land Stewardship Trust, who inspect and quantify the damage. If the pollution arises from outside the site the polluter has to pay the cost of the damage. Liability is determined by a tribunal of the Land Stewardship Trust.

How much pollution? Pollution becomes a problem when the Earth's ecosystems are unable to absorb the pollutants we produce without sustaining damage. We need a way to decide how much of each sort of pollutant to release each year. This requires not just a technical model of the impact of pollution but also an economic model that can aggregate the different sorts of costs and benefits, across time, of pollution reduction (abatement) – which requires a choice of discount rate.

Discounting. Stewardship is compatible with any rate of discounting, though its emphasis on fairness and the time-limited nature of stewardship should continually raise the issue and favour the long view. A green version of stewardship economy would choose a very low or zero rate of discounting.

Climate change

In an ownership economy....

The greenhouse effect was first described 150 years ago, and in 1980 the US National Academy of Sciences concluded in a report to Jimmy Carter that we could expect human-induced CO_2 emissions to bring about significant climate change. But it is only recently that we are beginning to contemplate taking any collective action to reduce the emissions of greenhouse gases. Is this simply one of a number of examples of our collective inability to address problems that challenge the status quo? Or is it connected with our way of seeing the Earth as something that can be owned and exploited?

Private property rights. The proximate cause of the problem is that the atmosphere has been treated as an open access regime, a sink into which everybody has been free to discharge pollutants. Our tentative response since the Kyoto Protocol was signed in 1997 has taken the promising form of 'cap and trade', which introduces private property rights in the form of tradable emissions permits.

Tragically, these permits have been gifted to existing polluters ('grandfathered') in a way that exactly parallels the way in which ownership of land has been gifted by the state to people or organisations whose favour it seeks. Polluters have profited from the gift and consumers have borne the cost.

Who suffers from climate change? The burden of climate change will be felt predominantly by poor countries, particularly those in Africa and those with significant amounts of land close to sea level like Bangladesh. In each country it is the poorest who will experience the most serious consequences. Amongst landowners it is the owners of the poorest land, most vulnerable to flooding and drought, who will suffer most.

In a stewardship economy….

We can only speculate whether, if a stewardship economy had been long established, the sense that we are all stewards not owners of the natural world would have led us to take action sooner. We might have responded to the 19th century challenge of air pollution not just by enacting the Clean Air Acts but also by setting up an Atmosphere Stewardship Trust (which we might now call the Sky Trust) to allocate private property rights in the atmosphere.

Private property rights. In a stewardship economy the Sky Trust determines the maximum permissible annual release of greenhouse gases; and auctions – not grandfathers – that number of tradable emissions permits.

Distribution of an Environmental Dividend. One source of opposition to environmental charges is the feeling that they constitute a 'stealth tax'. In view of the irreversible nature of established climate change the revenue from auctioning permits should be invested for future generations, for example to cope with (mitigate) the consequences. But because it is essential to enable people to accept the increase in the price of goods and services that are responsible for greenhouse gas emissions, I advocate the fiction that we are treating the atmosphere as a renewable resource, and so that the whole of the revenue from the auction of permits be distributed on an equal per capita basis as an Environmental Dividend. Those who use less than an equal share then receive a net income from the introduction of carbon permits, which makes contraction and convergence more acceptable.

Who suffers from climate change? Stewardship provides some degree of relief for those affected. Stewards whose land is permanently flooded, for example, will be relieved of stewardship fees or will receive 'negative fees' and will continue to receive as Universal Income a share of the market rent of the land that is not affected.

Energy

In an ownership economy....

Questions that have to be asked about each form of energy are: 'how much environmental damage is caused by its production and use?' and 'can its supply be sustained?'

True cost pricing. Neither the providers nor the consumers of energy have to pay for the damage they cause to the environment. This means that the price of energy does not reflect its true cost and we consume more than we should.

Ownership economies are beginning to introduce ways of bringing the costs of some forms of environmental damage, such as greenhouse gas emissions, into the costs of energy through taxation and the sale of emissions permits.

Rate of extraction. Governments fail to control the rate at which non-renewable resources are consumed. The wealth created by using non-renewable resources is largely squandered on current consumption rather than invested for the benefit of future generations, for example in alternative energy sources.

There is a strong body of opinion that we may already have passed Peak Oil, the time when the rate of extraction of oil begins to slow, supply falls and prices rise.

A simple economic model of fuel production suggests that the rising price of fuel will stimulate discovery and extraction. This simple model ignores the energy costs of fuel production – it is not helpful to extract fuel if it takes more energy to extract it than is released by its consumption.

Fuel poverty. The rich consume more energy per person than the poor but poor people spend a higher proportion of their income on energy, so the increased cost of energy is borne disproportionately by the poor. We have tried to deal with this problem by subsidising the fuel costs of the poor – for example the winter fuel payment for older people.

In a stewardship economy....

True cost pricing. One of the most important features of a stewardship economy, as it applies to the environment, is that firms and individuals that are responsible for environmental damage of any sort are responsible for paying for it. This is achieved in a variety of ways – for example requiring firms that introduce hydrocarbons into the economy to buy and surrender carbon permits to the Sky Trust; and requiring the operators of nuclear power plants to take out unlimited commercial insurance for environmental damage and contamination or diversion by terrorists. In this way the price of energy reflects its true cost including the cost to the environment and society; and this in turn increases the price and reduces the demand for goods and services that require energy in their production.

Rate of extraction. In a stewardship economy, a firm that extracts a non-renewable resource may be required to buy and surrender extraction permits at auction from the Oil and Minerals Stewardship Trust. This payment reduces the incentive to deplete stocks rapidly, and if the Trust believes that stocks of a non-renewable resource are being run down too quickly it can reduce the number of extraction permits it makes available each year.

Environmental Dividend. As mentioned in the previous section on climate change I propose that the revenue from the auction of carbon permits be distributed as an equal Environmental Dividend, rather than investing it for the benefit of future generations as would ideally happen. The effect of this is to redistribute wealth from high users to low users of energy, which in general means from the wealthy to the poor. This turns the regressive effect of increasing the price of energy into a progressive package of charges plus Environmental Dividend which ensures that the poor benefit as the wealthy bear more than an equal share of the cost.

Countryside

In an ownership economy....

Agriculture is inevitably shaped by the demands of the economy, which are often at odds with good husbandry.

Economics. Agriculture, with its dependence on the weather and the generosity of nature, is an uncertain business. Tenant farmers often find it difficult to make a living, while agricultural landowners own an appreciating asset that benefits from tax exemptions – particularly from tax on fuel, Capital Gains Tax and Inheritance Tax.

Subsidies. In high-consumption ownership economies the state supports agriculture by paying subsidies, which over time have moved away from subsidising production to subsidising environmental management. Subsidies have a number of problems – they burden the taxpayer; benefit the landowner by increasing the market rent and market value of land; distort international trade; harm low-consumption economies; but fail to improve conditions for tenant farmers as, even when paid to the tenant, they cause rents to rise.

Farming. Agriculture is shaped by the current low prices of petrochemicals and energy, which do not represent the true cost of the environmental damage they cause. These prices favour capital-intensive rather than labour-intensive production methods. Transport, particularly air freight, is cheaper than its true cost price and this increases competition from overseas producers which in turn reduces the price available to local producers.

Agriculture in ownership economies provides little employment on the land and an uncertain income for the tenant farmer. Production is intensive, and requires high inputs of fertilisers, fuel, heat and specialised machinery. Monoculture increases the risk of disease in crops and animal populations and output is dependent on the use of pesticides and antibiotics.

In a stewardship economy….

The economic forces acting on agriculture in a stewardship economy are very different.

The cost of land. There is nothing to be gained from renting out unimproved land in a stewardship economy (though leasing buildings still provides a viable business model). Most farmers are stewards not tenants. The cost of land for a steward farmer in a stewardship economy is the same as the cost for a tenant farmer in an ownership society – the stewardship fee is equal to the market rent of the land.

Economics. It is difficult to predict how profitable farms would be in a stewardship economy. Food prices are higher as they reflect the true cost of fuel and other agricultural inputs. Farmers are exempt from many forms of taxation in ownership economies, so would not benefit as much as other businesses from the removal of these taxes. The economics of farming would probably hinge, as it does in ownership economies, on the level of subsidy.

Subsidy. In a stewardship economy the government does not pay production subsidies or set-aside payments or make intervention purchases. But society needs agriculture to operate profitably so that it provides security of food supply and manages the landscape.

This means that the Land Stewardship Trust must be prepared to accept negative bids for stewardship fees for agricultural land when there are no positive bids. This provides an automatic subsidy, the level of which is determined in the market.

Farming. Most farmers are stewards rather than tenants, so farms are smaller. With higher prices for fuel and fertiliser, agriculture would become more labour-intensive and more organic, with less emphasis on animal husbandry and more on horticulture.

Chapter 8 Economy

Business and charities

In an ownership economy....

Profitability. Corporation Tax and VAT reduce profitability, and taxes generally reduce the level of economic activity and growth.

Labour market flexibility. For a worker to achieve a certain level of take-home pay their employer will be paying 2–3 times this amount after Income Tax, National Insurance, sick pay and so on are taken into account. These payroll taxes make it expensive for an employer to take on employees.

Red tape. It's not just the financial impact of taxes that impose a burden on business. Firms are required to act as tax-collectors (for VAT, PAYE and National Insurance), administrators of maternity and sick pay schemes, providers of pensions and in some countries of health care – all of which adds up to a significant burden of red tape and complexity as well as cost. The tax system also requires firms to prepare and submit accounts that are not in the form they need to understand their business; and to adapt their business to minimise tax liabilities rather than maximise their pre-tax profits.

Land values. In our current ownership world, some businesses and individuals move to tax havens like Jersey or Monaco, even though it may be very expensive to buy or to rent property there – land values are enhanced by the low-tax environment.

Charities receive a state subsidy in the form of relief from Income Tax on charitable donations and as a result of exemption from the Non-Domestic (Business) Rates and (in general) Corporation Tax. This enables them to achieve more of their charitable aims and confers a competitive advantage where charities are in competition with private sector firms.

In a stewardship economy….

Stewardship fees. A business pays the market rent for the land it uses – either to a landlord or as a stewardship fee.

Profitability. A business that rents its property in an ownership economy may be more profitable in a stewardship economy as the cost of its land is the same while it may pay reduced or zero Corporation Tax, VAT or National Insurance contributions.

The profitability of a business that owns its property in an ownership economy is broadly the same in a stewardship economy. It may pay reduced taxes, but any reduction is offset by the requirement to pay stewardship fees.

A business that rents out land in an ownership economy is less profitable as it has to pay stewardship fees on its land.

Labour market flexibility. Businesses find it easier to take on new employees as payroll taxes, and perhaps wages, are lower.

A Universal Income makes it is less necessary to protect workers from dismissal, but it also improves their bargaining position as they have less incentive to accept unsatisfactory jobs.

Red tape. All businesses benefit from reduction in the red tape that an ownership economy imposes.

Land values. During transition as stewardship fees rise, conventional taxes may fall and the market rent of land increase, so that and stewardship fees rise further, making additional tax cuts possible in a virtuous circle.

Charities. There are challenges for charities in a stewardship economy. A charity is not exempt from paying stewardship fees and, depending on the degree to which taxes are obviated, has less or no competitive advantage over private sector firms. To counteract these challenges the state will need to provide some form of direct subsidy to charities, for example in proportion to the revenue that the charity raises.

Money and banking

In an ownership economy....

Fractional reserve banking. The right to designate legal tender is the prerogative of the state. In ownership economies central banks issue coin and notes but the creation of the remaining 97 per cent of money is franchised to the commercial banks through the fractional reserve system.

The commercial banks create money by making loans, the interest on which provides the holders of the franchise with a state subsidy of over £20 billion a year in the UK. This is a failure of imagination by the state, and the consequence of an historical accident in the way that monopoly rights have been created – not unlike land ownership.

House price bubbles. The banking and international finance system collapsed in 2008 as a result of the bursting of a bubble in house prices in America. Any policy that had checked the growth of this bubble would have reduced the severity of the subsequent recession. Instead, banks had expanded the money supply by lending against the collateral of over-optimistic property valuations, further inflating the growth in prices.

Too big to fail? Once the bubble had burst the value of land-backed financial derivatives fell, threatening banks, insurers and the global financial system. Governments felt compelled to rescue institutions that were judged to be 'too big to fail', at the cost of more than $9 trillion to their taxpayers.

Depositors in retail banks need risk-free banking, and so close regulation and a credible deposit guarantee scheme.

Shares (equity) provide the loss-absorbing part of a bank's liability structure and shareholders, not the state, must bear any losses. Regulation must ensure that banks are capable of re-capitalising themselves by converting their own debt into equity when threatened with insolvency – they have proved to be 'too big to rescue'.

In a stewardship economy....

Full-reserve banking. The central bank takes on the role of issuing money into the economy – full-reserve banking. (The Bank of England has issued money directly, quantitative easing, since 2009 because retail banks have not created enough money for the economy to function.) The monetary policy committee of the central bank decides how much money needs to be issued into the economy in order to control inflation and manage economic growth and authorises the government to spend this money into circulation. You might not want to trust the state with the right to 'print money', but the banks have proved to have too narrow an interest to play this role in the financial system.

The New Economics Foundation proposes that banks provide risk-free custody of deposits, with payment facilities, in 'transaction accounts'. They would provide separately managed 'investment accounts', which would be used by the bank to make loans and from which withdrawals could be made only after a notice period. Investment accounts would carry a risk, as they would automatically be converted into equity if the bank became insolvent; so the banks could re-capitalise themselves without requiring taxpayer bailouts.

These arrangements prevent the bank from amplifying boom and bust, allow the central bank to control the money supply directly and do not require the creation of widespread indebtedness to provide a medium of exchange.

House price bubbles. The banking system is more robust in a stewardship economy. There is no risk of a property price bubble; and banks have to base their lending on the borrower's ability to repay, not on the collateral value of land.

Avoiding sovereign debt. As the economy grows the money supply needs to grow as well. The government spends into circulation the new money, which it would otherwise have had to raise on the bond market.

Efficiency in the short term

In an ownership economy....

Orthodox economics takes as its starting point a view of the economy as a system at, or close to, equilibrium. There is no guarantee that, in an economy at equilibrium, aggregate demand is high enough to provide full employment. How efficiently does the market allocate land, labour and capital?

Land. In an ownership economy there is over-investment in land. There is also extensive under-use, or inefficient use, with significant amounts of land held by people who do not use it productively. The land market itself is inefficient, providing inadequate information and enabling speculation to mask the underlying price signals. The tax system does nothing to counteract this, and indeed exacerbates it with exemptions for empty properties and taxes that discourage transactions and development.

Capital. Over-investment in land leads to under-investment in capital goods, and so to under-production. This is compounded by Income Tax on savings which discourages investment, VAT which discourages adding value and Corporation Tax which discourages profitable enterprise.

Labour. Income Tax on earnings and National Insurance contributions increase the cost of employing labour. The current benefit system, essential as it is in reducing poverty, discourages people from taking up part-time and low-paid work and training (the unemployment trap).

Taxes. When taxes are removed, as in the Enterprise Zones of the 1980s, it is the market rent of land that rises not the levels of wages or profits. Conventional taxes reduce economic activity and reduce market rents.

This distorts the allocation of resources, and the overall burden of taxation creates a deadweight loss to the economy. This is a central reason why ownership economies experience unnecessarily low rates of economic growth.

In a stewardship economy....

Land. In a stewardship economy the land market is more efficient than it is in an ownership economy, as information is more readily available and there is no speculation. Land is put to more efficient use than in an ownership economy because each steward feels a regular financial incentive to put it to its best use, or to dispose of it, each time they pay the stewardship fee. The strongest incentive falls on the land that is least well used, encouraging more uniform development.

Capital. Savings in a stewardship economy are not invested in land and are available for investment in production.

Labour. People have an incentive to work even when this is part-time, voluntary or at a low rate of pay because the Universal Income is not withdrawn when they work. Labour is used more efficiently.

Freedom from taxes. A stewardship economy benefits from the reduction or absence of conventional taxes, including reduction or avoidance of the specific distortions of particular taxes, such as taxes on labour that reduce investment in labour-intensive activities and taxes on savings that reduce investment in capital. It reduces or removes the deadweight loss of taxation, so the level of economic activity is higher. The single most far-reaching economic consequence of a fully developed stewardship economy is this liberation from conventional taxation.

As conventional taxes are reduced during transition to a stewardship economy, the market rent of land will rise. The extent of the rise depends on how much people really want land compared with goods and services – on the relative elasticities of demand. There is reason to expect that competition for land would remain strong and that market rents would rise by as much as the taxes fell – or by an even greater amount as the economy grows with the removal of the deadweight loss of taxation.

Investment and long-term growth

In an ownership economy....

Investment. The economy has grown in a spectacular way over the last two centuries, fuelled by cheap energy. This has required investment in innovation and new technologies.

Some forms of savings may be used to invest in new productive enterprise – new issues of shares, corporate bonds or government bonds for example, and bank deposits. But the purchase of land, or second-hand assets like existing shares, transfers wealth from one owner to another and does not constitute investment in production.

The biggest expenditure for most households is their home – land plus a second-hand building. This leaves them in debt and reduces their capacity to invest in enterprise.

Economic growth. Unlike most governments in ownership economies, we should not assume that economic growth is desirable. We are not the first civilisation to be hastening our own end by the environmental destruction caused by a successful economy, though we are the first to do so on a global scale. And even when growth provides us with material wealth it fails to furnish our lives with happiness – indeed growth detracts from happiness when it increases inequalities in wealth.

The problem is that, in ownership economies, we can't do without economic growth. The reason is that the wealth the economy creates is distributed mainly though employment (or self-employment). As technology advances, labour productivity increases and jobs are destroyed. Growth is needed, not to create wealth but to replace the jobs that technological development destroys. Dynamic modelling shows that zero economic growth would create poverty and unemployment unless it was accompanied by measures that share out the available work and redistribute income.

In a stewardship economy....

Investment. Land is acquired and held by making regular payments not by outright purchase. One consequence is that there is less household debt, and more savings are available for investment in productive enterprise. This increase in investment, combined with the removal of the deadweight loss of taxation, enables a stewardship economy to grow faster than an ownership economy.

Economic growth. One of the important challenges in any economy is to prevent damage to the environment by economic activity. In a stewardship economy firms have to pay the true cost of using the environment, and this reduces economic growth. Stewardship of land and stewardship of the environment need to be advanced together – on their own, one may risk too much growth and the other too little.

The good news is that setting limits to economic growth in a stewardship economy does not need to threaten the quality and happiness of our lives. Everybody receives a Universal Income, whether or not they work, though this may not on its own be enough to avoid poverty. People with only a part-time job, or even with no job, share in the wealth that is created. The Universal Income makes it possible to tolerate reduced or perhaps zero economic growth, if that is what is needed.

This means that the need for economic growth that creates jobs is much less intense than in an ownership economy. People may still want to consume more; but as they become freer to work in situations that are satisfying and have less need to compete in a more equal society, it is possible that the pressure to consume may fall. Even if economic growth is maintained it will, as a result of environmental charges, consist of growth in goods and services that are less environmentally damaging than the mix provided at the moment.

Boom, bust and inflation

In an ownership economy....

Economic activity does not grow smoothly – superimposed on the long-term growth are medium-term swings between boom and bust. At times labour and capital are well-utilised; at other times there is under-investment, under-use of land and unemployment. The pattern of this quasi-cyclical change is not-quite-regular but not-quite-random.

Housing bubbles. During an upswing people become more confident about the future, and the prices of assets – particularly shares and land – rise. Expectation of further price increases fuels further investment, speculation, borrowing and expansion of the money supply until a point is reached when recognition dawns that these asset prices are unsustainable. The bubble bursts, asset prices fall, borrowing is reduced, the money supply shrinks, aggregate demand falls, and the economy slows.

When a land price bubble bursts it is much more likely to trigger a significant economic downturn than when a share price bubble bursts. If we could prevent land price bubbles, then the associated economic downturns could be prevented.

Before the credit crunch of 2007, governments and central bankers believed that the economy was stable because consumer price inflation was under control. Policy-makers failed to remember the consequences of previous housing bubbles and there was no consensus that there might be a need to curb inflation in the price of assets, particularly land. But even if they had wanted to take action, their principal policy option – raising interest rates to reduce the money supply – would have further damaged the manufacturing sector, particularly its capacity to export. And it would have failed to reduce 'investment' in land that was providing returns of over 20 per cent per year, far higher than the level at which it would have been possible to set interest rates.

In a stewardship economy....

Stable house prices. A stewardship economy stabilises the prices of houses and other properties. The price of buildings rises at no more than the rate of price inflation in the building trade, and the market value of land itself is zero.

There is no speculation in land. There are no housing bubbles and none of the consequent busts and economic downturns. Land is held for use not investment.

A stewardship economy with its stable land prices is not free from quasi-cyclical changes as people express their optimism and pessimism by buying and selling other assets like shares. But some economic downturns, like the one that began in 2008, would not occur or would not be as severe.

Reducing boom and bust. There are other reasons why a stewardship economy is cushioned from economic downturns. Monetary reform stabilises the money supply by preventing the banks from creating and destroying money; and the deadweight loss of conventional taxes is reduced or removed, which improves the efficiency of the land market, the labour market and the economy as a whole.

Increased demand. In addition, the re-distributive effect of the Universal Income increases the income of poorer people, who are more likely than the wealthy to spend it on current consumption, and this increases aggregate demand.

Inflation. Stewardship fees are not passed on through higher prices to the consumer, so stewardship of land is not inflationary. New environmental charges are intended to raise prices and do lead to consumer price inflation; but those who use less than an equal share of the environment find that this is counterbalanced by receiving a net payment from the Environmental Dividend. During transition it is important not to adjust monetary policy in response to price rises caused by environmental charges.

Chapter 9   Distribution of wealth

Universal Income

In an ownership economy....

In high-consumption ownership economies the state re-distributes wealth to poorer people by means of contributory benefits, non-contributory benefits and Tax Credits.

Work and unemployment.   Benefits that are conditional on availability for work create an 'unemployment trap' that can make it illogical for an unemployed person to work. The level of benefit sets a floor below which it makes no sense to engage in work, particularly when the costs of work clothes, travel and childcare are taken into consideration. And the combination of Income Tax with withdrawal of benefits means that for every extra pound that a person earns they may lose more than 90 pence – the 'poverty trap'.

Sickness and disability. Benefits for people who are sick or disabled require beneficiaries to delay their return to work until they are 100 per cent fit for work, rather than gaining confidence and health working part-time.

Women are often ineligible for full National Insurance benefits because of an incomplete contribution record.

Couples. Couples who co-habit receive lower levels of benefit than those who live apart, providing an incentive to maintain separate households.

Children. One fifth of children in the UK live in poverty in spite of the introduction of Tax Credits.

Pensions.   Pensions are eroded by Income Tax.   People are discouraged from accumulating savings that may make them ineligible for means-tested Pension Credit.

Burden of taxation. The tax-benefit system, as a whole, transfers wealth from the rich to the poor. But the tax system itself takes a greater proportion of the income of the poor than of the wealthy.

In a stewardship economy….

A stewardship fee is a charge not a tax, but it can usefully be compared with the taxes found in ownership economies.

Universal Income provides everybody with a small independent income that is determined by the total stewardship fees collected less the government's expenses – not by the needs of its recipients. There is no means testing.

Work and unemployment. Universal Income is paid even when its recipient is in work. People have an incentive to work even when this is low-paid or part-time, as they receive the whole of their pay with little or no tax and no withdrawal of benefits. This avoids fraudulent benefit claims while working.

Sickness, disability and carers benefits are the same in a liberal version of stewardship as they are at present.

Women receive the same Universal Income as men.

Couples. The Universal Income is paid to individuals not to families or households and is therefore not reduced when couples or other groups of people share accommodation.

Children. Children receive an independent income – each child brings its own income stream.

Pensions. Universal Income is paid whatever level of savings or income a pensioner has. The reduction or removal of taxes on pension contributions and payments encourage saving.

Burden of taxation. Stewardship generally transfers wealth from the rich to the poor because wealthy people usually have larger homes in more desirable locations than poorer people, and so pay higher stewardship fees while receiving the same level of Universal Income.

Special consideration needs to be given during transition to people who live on low incomes in areas of high land value, particularly those who live alone.

Inequalities

In an ownership economy....

Causes of inequality. Computer models of even simple, stylised trading economies generate inequalities of wealth that are caused largely by chance rather than by either exploitation or differences between the attributes of the players. The observed inequalities in human economies are inevitable unless we take measures to reduce them.

In ownership economies these inequalities are reinforced by land ownership. Tenants have to pay rent while owners receive it (and owner-occupiers are exempt from payment).

Effects of inequality. There is evidence, albeit contested, that countries with a more equal distribution of income suffer from higher rates of suicide but benefit on measures of homicide, discrimination (by race, ethnicity, gender and class), violent crime, domestic violence, obesity, drug and alcohol dependence, teenage pregnancy, social cohesion, educational attainment, trust and life expectancy. Levels of inequality vary enough among states in the USA to be associated with a five-fold difference in homicide rates.

Happiness is higher in high-consumption economies than in low-consumption economies, as people have the basic necessities of life. But people in wealthier high-consumption economies are no happier than people in poorer ones. Almost everybody is healthier and happier in a more equal society (with the possible exception of the very richest). The way to increase health and happiness may not be to increase per capita GDP but to reduce inequalities.

Income Tax. Income Tax takes a greater proportion of the income of the rich than of the poor – it is a progressive tax. But if it is considered along with the closely related Capital Gains Tax with its exemptions for home ownership, it is regressive – it takes a greater proportion of the income of the poor than of the rich.

In a stewardship economy....

Re-distribution. People with the most wealth and highest incomes are likely to occupy high-value properties. They will contribute more in stewardship fees than people with low-value properties. Everybody benefits more or less equally from government expenditure on public goods and from receipt of the Universal Income. The combination of stewardship fees and Universal Income transfers income from people living on sites with high per capita land values to people living on sites with low per capita land values.

A tax on wealth has greater power to reduce inequalities than a tax on income, as wealth is more concentrated in the population than income.

It is possible for the rich to avoid the redistribution by moving to low-value properties, but few are likely to do so as the location of their home is so important to most people. If they did so, it would increase the diversity of these areas.

Environmental charges redistribute wealth from people who use more than an equal share of environmental resources to those who use less than an equal share. It is the rich who generally use more than their equal share, though the high cost of energy for heating the home is felt particularly by poorer people – which suggests the need for regulation of landlords and subsidies for home insulation.

Effects. Wealth and income are likely to be more equally distributed than in ownership economies. As a consequence, stewardship economies are likely to be healthier, happier, more socially cohesive, less discriminatory and less violent.

Income Tax. Although Income Tax in a mature Stewardship Economy, it could be retained during transition to ensure that inequalities are minimised. It might then be phased out as soon as the rates of pay of the highest-paid and lowest-paid converge.

Chapter 10 The state

The role of the state

In an ownership economy....

There are many views about what is the proper role for the state and what is the proper role for private contracts and markets. Jane Jacobs (1992) explores the value systems that are deployed in the world of work and distinguishes between two moral syndromes. One, the contractual or commercial syndrome, is appropriate in situations where organisations are seeking mutually beneficial voluntary agreements. The other, the guardian syndrome, is appropriate for tasks that protect a society's territory and integrity. Contractual occupations include trade, production and the pursuit of science. Guardian occupations include the military, the legal and criminal justice systems, regulatory bodies and public health. It is a guardian function to maintain the context within which contractual functions can flourish – including the establishment of property rights, enforcement of the law of contract, and regulation of the financial system.

Jane Jacobs suggests that these moral syndromes need to be kept separate, and that problems arise when commercial morality is applied to guardian functions (e.g., when planning permission is sold) or when guardian morality is applied to contractual functions (e.g., when a command economy determines production). She describes the Mafia as a 'monstrous hybrid' that uses guardian morality to manage commercial activity. Contemporary examples of hybrids include the Private Finance Initiative and the banking system, both of which have enabled private sector firms to privatise the profits and socialise the risk.

This analysis provides a language for thinking about the role of the state. It suggests that there should be a clear separation, with the state taking on many guardian functions and the private sector taking on contractual functions.

In a stewardship economy….

Choice of roles for the state. The nature of the common good is always contested and has to be decided by political processes.

Stewardship is compatible with the state taking on a very wide range of roles. It is not a simple prescription for an ideal state, but a platform on which a wide variety of different societies could flourish.

There are a certain number of functions that a state would find unavoidable if it makes use of stewardship – including the guardian functions of defence, legislation, law enforcement (including enforcing property rights and contracts), valuing land and improvements, transferring properties at auction, distributing Universal Income and land use planning.

Government spending. One of the challenges in a stewardship economy is how to restrain state spending. Higher spending does not lead to higher taxes but to lower levels of Universal Income, which is difficult for electors to identify. A stewardship economy needs some way to hold the government properly to account for its levels of spending, for example legally binding manifesto commitments to budgets.

Allocation of monopoly rights. Titles to land and to the environment are examples of monopoly rights that are granted by the state. Allocating these rights by auction rather than as an act of patronage brings the benefit of efficient allocation as well as generating revenue. A similar approach may be applied to other state-granted monopolies and franchises.

Transport and utilities

In an ownership economy....

An effective transport system provides the basis for an economy based on specialisation and trade. But the price mechanism operates very imperfectly to guide decisions about travel and about investment in transport infrastructure because it fails to recognise and take account of significant costs and benefits of transport provision.

Costs. The cost of congestion, noise, pollution and greenhouse gas emissions are borne by the general population or by the travelling public, not by transport providers. The resulting price distortions promote pollution and congestion and favour private over public transport. We have designed these consequences into the transport system through the economic approach we have taken.

Benefits. When a new transport link is built, it provides benefits not just to those who travel but also to landowners.

Early investors in the canals and railways, like those in the channel tunnel, lost much of their investment because the operating revenues were not high enough to repay the costs of development. It was landowners, not investors, who profited from their new-found ability to get crops and minerals speedily and cheaply to market. City centres and their suburbs rely on good transport links for their symbiosis, causing increases in the market rents in both.

It is unusual for the providers of new transport infrastructure to benefit from the increased market rents, but exceptions have included the American railways, the London Metropolitan line and the Hong Kong mass transit railway.

The need for subsidy. When developers cannot make a profit the state has to subsidise the construction, and even operation, of transport infrastructure. This requires taxation with its deadweight loss, which damages the economy and limits the investment available.

In a stewardship economy....

True cost prices. The user of any form of transport pays a price that reflects its true cost, including the costs of congestion, greenhouse emissions and other pollution. This discourages private transport, which is less fuel-efficient than public transport and causes more congestion.

Transport Stewardship Trusts. Each mode of transport is managed by its own Transport Stewardship Trust, which holds a network of land in trust and manages it by regulation or by selling time-limited private property rights. The Roads Stewardship Trust, for example, can choose to sell permits for road journeys wherever there is congestion. Transport operating companies bid for, or request the lowest subsidy for, the right to operate trains, boats and buses on the relevant network. Airport landing and take-off slots are allocated by auction rather than gifted to the company that has made use of them in the past.

Self-funding infrastructure. Stewardship can stimulate the construction and operation of transport infrastructure, by collecting the increased market rent of land that benefits from the infrastructure. The proportion of the stewardship fees for that land that is attributed to the infrastructure can then be reserved (hypothecated) to pay for its construction, and if necessary, its operation, which may enable it to be self-funding. Stewardship fees do not create any deadweight loss for the economy, so the government can invest in infrastructure as long as the benefits outweigh its costs – just as the private sector would.

The same approach can be used to fund the provision of other forms of infrastructure – the supply systems for water, electricity, broadband etc. The provision of these services to properties increases the market rent of the land at these sites in the same way that the provision of transport does.

Public services

In an ownership economy….

Political choices. Libertarians believe that the state inevitably limits individual freedom, but right-libertarians somewhat paradoxically also believe that the state should defend the existing regime of property rights. Socialists, with their concern for the well-being of the whole of society, tend to advocate an active role for the state; though this is not inevitable as it is possible to influence the overall behaviour of a complex system without imposing a design.

Public goods. Orthodox economics suggests that the state needs to provide 'public goods' – goods that are consumed by society as a whole rather than by individuals. The benefit of a public good is spread amongst the whole community – like street lighting or defence. Individuals do not purchase a share of it, and if we rely on market mechanisms alone it will be supplied either not at all, or in smaller quantities than is optimal. Many public goods are guardian functions – for example defence, public health, regulation – and most people recognise these as appropriate roles for the state to take on.

The term 'market failure' is used to describe a wider group of situations in which there is an inefficient allocation of resources. This may cause goods and services to be supplied in sub-optimal amounts.

Taxation. Public goods require taxation and conventional taxes create a deadweight loss. From an ethical perspective they take from people what is rightly theirs – their income from work and investments. This means that there are always political choices to be made about how much the state should do to provide public goods and to correct market failures. Political parties coalesce around these choices about spending and taxation.

In a stewardship economy....

Political choices. Political differences are alive and well in a stewardship economy. Stewardship economies of different political complexions would make very different choices about what public goods to provide and how to fund them.

Some choices are very similar to those in ownership economies, such as whether people pay for their own health and social care or whether we share the risk collectively.

Self-funding possibilities. Other choices can be made in a stewardship economy from a new set of possibilities, such as the self-funding of infrastructure and amenities like parks. In a similar way the increased stewardship fees of homes in the catchment areas of good schools could be used to fund the provision of education – it is a political choice whether this should benefit the good school itself or the neighbouring schools that are struggling. The presence of a university in a city is known to stimulate the local economy, and the component of local stewardship fees attributed to this stimulation could be used to subsidise the university.

Possibilities offered by the Universal Income. More radical possibilities are opened up when people, including schoolchildren, have their own Universal Income. Here it is much easier to imagine schools charging fees and still providing equitable access. The Universal Income could reduce the amount of debt incurred by students and so make it easier for people to undertake education and training at any stage in their lives. It could also support the reciprocal networks of gift exchange that sustain community through voluntary work, caring for family and friends, and the creation of works of art.

Another new possibility offered by stewardship is the option of deducting a fine from the Universal Income at source, thereby reducing imprisonment for non-payment of fines.

Chapter 11 Global economy

International issues

In an ownership economy....

Free trade. Where there is free movement of goods and capital, some areas and groups of people prosper at the expense of others. Generally, it is consumers, businesses and highly skilled workers who benefit, and less skilled workers who suffer. Free trade areas, like the European Union, have to put in place transfers of wealth to support those who suffer in order to prevent them from erecting tariff and subsidy barriers out of self-interest. These transfers often take the form of time-limited regeneration programmes.

Population movements. The theory of free trade assumes that people as well as goods and capital are mobile. People living in low-consumption countries recognise that they have a greater opportunity to make economic progress if they migrate to a higher-consumption economy. These movements can be beneficial to both economies but may be disruptive to the lives of the migrants and put the culture of both countries under stress, particularly when migration is on a large scale.

The environment. There is a pressing need for international institutions that have the legitimacy and tools to resolve environmental challenges on a global scale.

Territorial disputes. There are many outstanding territorial disputes, often related to the ownership of natural resources. These are only likely to intensify over the next century, as resource scarcity (particularly water and oil) intensifies and as climate change makes more land incapable of supporting existing population levels. We have only poorly developed institutions for resolving these disputes, and these generally rely on the arbitration of competing historical claims reinforced by the threat of military power.

In a stewardship economy….

There are additional benefits when stewardship is introduced at an international or even global scale.

International Stewardship is the practice of sharing between nations the revenue from stewardship fees and environmental charges. It provides automatic unconditional transfer payments from areas of high per capita land values to areas of low per capita land values, and from countries with a big environmental footprint to those with a small one.

Free Trade. International Stewardship ensures that countries and people that benefit from free trade compensate those that do not. As all countries then benefit from free trade, none has an incentive to impose tariffs or to dump produce.

Population movements. International Stewardship provides everybody with a share of the wealth generated by the global economy without their needing to move to another country.

The environment. Stewardship provides institutions that are appropriate to tackling international and global environmental issues – International Watershed Trusts and a Global Sky Trust for example.

Sharing the revenue from environmental charges as an International Environmental Dividend provides a way to compensate and engage low-consumption economies in international environmental protection agreements that would otherwise not be in their interests.

Territorial disputes. An occupier is less likely to claim territory and natural resources when they have to pay their newly acquired market rents into an international fund. A fair balance of present liabilities is more likely to lead to peaceful resolution than disputes about historical claims. And stewardship offers a market-based approach to resolving disputes.

Low-consumption economies

In an ownership economy….

The degree of inequality between poor countries and rich countries is grotesque and increasing.

Institutions. Many of the economic difficulties in low-consumption economies are related to institutional and structural problems. People occupying land to which they do not have secure title are at risk of eviction by the state, intimidation and coercion; and land tenure systems frequently discriminate against women. Secure title to land is an important requirement for economic development, as a means of securing property against arbitrary seizure and as an asset that can be used as collateral when borrowing to finance a business.

Resource rents. Economic explanations go some way towards explaining the 'curse of oil' that impoverishes many resource-rich countries, but more important are the corruption and civil wars that frequently arise from struggles to control the ability to exploit natural resources and the wealth they confer (resource rents).

Aid has provided low-consumption economies with many benefits, particularly in emergency situations. But the amount of multilateral aid has been small, and bilateral (government to government) aid has often served the needs of the donors rather than the recipients.

Trade may offer a more substantial and sustainable basis for reducing inequalities, but high-consumption economies have been reluctant to abandon the subsidies to their own producers, particularly in the agricultural sector, and to remove tariff barriers. This protectionism is harmful to global trade and to low-consumption economies. A new threat is the purchase of large tracts of agricultural land and natural resources by foreign corporations and sovereign wealth funds that are seeking to secure stable supplies of food, biofuels and raw materials.

In a stewardship economy....

The economic fortunes of low-consumption stewardship economies are likely to be much better than low-consumption ownership economies.

Economics. Low-consumption economies benefit internally from stewardship in the same ways that high-consumption economies do. They have more efficient land and labour markets and suffer less, if at all, from the deadweight loss of taxation. Stewardship fees offer a secure source of revenue either for government expenditure or to fund a Universal Income.

Institutions. One of the earliest benefits of stewardship is the strengthening of institutions. The apparatus needed to collect stewardship fees requires the government to set up a land register in which the title to all property is recorded. This unambiguous, secure title offers people both in agricultural areas and in slums greater freedom from insecurity and coercion, and the opportunity to improve their properties and to develop a more secure way of life.

Stewardship is close in spirit to traditional forms of land tenure in which land is held as common property. It should not be used to draw indigenous peoples inappropriately into private property and the money economy.

Resource rents. Stewardship provides a way to capture the market rent of natural resources in a transparent way. This offers the possibility of reduced corruption and violence, and better governance. The revenue can provide an Environmental Dividend for every man, woman and child.

International Stewardship provides regular transfers to low-consumption economies that relieve poverty, stimulate the local economy and reduce outward migration. High-consumption economies do not need to protect their domestic industries with tariff and subsidy barriers as wealth is distributed there as Universal Income as well as wages.

In summary: Stewardship is not a blueprint for a single way to organise society, but an alternative to one of the unspoken assumptions that underlie the present arrangements. The form stewardship takes would depend on a wide range of political choices.

An established stewardship economy does not extend any financial privilege to people or organisations that have an historical claim on the Earth and its resources. Whoever wants a site has to pay the stewardship fee and go on paying it. In a variety of ways, we all benefit – from the reduction or abolition of conventional taxes with their deadweight loss; the provision of a Universal Income; the funding of transport and other infrastructure by those whose land benefits; the redistribution of wealth between individuals, neighbourhoods, regions and countries; the prevention of housing (land) price bubbles with their associated economic crashes and negative equity; and protection of the environment.

One of the major challenges for government is how to make good decisions that take into account their impact across the whole of the economy and society. There is an understandable temptation to think, and to make decisions, in departmental silos. It is unlikely that anybody would take the political risk of making a transition to stewardship for any one reason on its own – it is the whole package that is compelling.

That is why Part III has sought to sketch a picture of what a whole stewardship economy might be like. This is a summary of material included in other books in the series.

PART IV STEWARDSHIP – WHY AND HOW

If we are to grasp the benefits of stewardship that were described in Part III, we need to be assured that stewardship is fair, efficient and capable of being made to work. These issues are discussed in the next two chapters.

Chapter 12 Why it's fair and efficient

Ownership of the *things* that we make seems fair to most people. If I have made a table, it seems reasonable that I should have the right to use it and dispose of it as I please – to own it. When a firm manufactures tables, it, too, owns them. Production justifies the acquisition of property.

If I then sell a table, the purchaser has a fair claim to own it. Here, ownership is justified by tracing a chain of voluntary transactions from the present owner back to the producer.

Stewardship is based on a clear distinction between artefacts (the things that we make) and the natural world (that which is provided in nature). In a stewardship economy, artefacts are held in ownership while the natural world is held in stewardship.

This chapter outlines why stewardship is:

o   a fair alternative to ownership of the land (efficiency was covered in Chapter 6)

o   an efficient and fair way to manage the environment

o   an efficient and fair way to raise revenue

o   an efficient and fair benefit system.

It provides a summary of material that is presented at greater depth in other books in the series.

Property in land

Fairness

In an ownership economy....

In an ownership economy, land can be owned in the same way as artefacts. The justification is that a chain of transactions leads back ultimately to somebody who claims 'secure title' – not as the maker of the land but as a result of one of two possible actions. One is 'first occupancy' – that were the first person to occupy the land. The other is 'first use' – that they were the first person to apply their labour and make use of it. Frequently these actions are combined – the settler who occupies 'un-owned' land, stakes it out, builds a homestead and cultivates the land. Surely, they own this land just as certainly as I own my table?

Naturally they own the buildings, fences, land drains and crops. These are things that they have created or produced and have the right to own. But is it really fair for them to claim ownership of the land itself, in perpetuity, just because they were the first to occupy or use it?

It's as though a traveller on a train gets aboard, sits down and claims ownership of the seat. Generations later their descendants are renting the seat out to new passengers.

In reality, claims to the ownership of land are much more tenuous even than this. In law the owner of land is the person who has the best, not the perfect, title. The idea that a chain of transactions actually links us to an original settler of unoccupied land is frankly fanciful. Where the chain can be identified it leads back to warfare, conquest, violence or the arbitrary action of a ruler. How many land claims in the UK date back to the enclosures, the clearances, the dissolution of the monasteries, or the Norman Conquest? In many other countries the discontinuity is much more recent. It's as if we are renting that seat on the train from the descendant of a highway robber who ejected the previous occupant.

In a stewardship economy....

Stewardship provides a fair way to allocate the natural world, based in current reality not in historical claims.

One way to think about the nature of a just and fair society is to conduct thought experiments that use the device of a 'social contract', an implied agreement about the social arrangements in a society.

We all bring to these experiments our experience of a particular set of endowments and preferences. Our contribution is likely, for example, to be affected by whether we belong to the class of landowner or landless. One way to try to avoid this bias is to ask what social contract we would favour if we were placed behind a 'veil of ignorance' that obscured the position, condition and preferences that we would have in the society in question.

If we were designing from scratch a society in which we might or might not end up as potential owners of some part of the natural world, we would surely not base ownership claims on either first occupancy or on first use. A compact between the current steward and the rest of us, in which they compensate us for excluding us from that land or aspect of the environment, must surely be fairer and preferable.

The claim that stewardship is a fair way to organise an ideal society leaves open the question of how to make a fair transition from an ownership economy. The fundamental principle that underlies the proposed transition mechanism is full respect for all property rights that exist at the onset of transition (Chapter 14). Since the current market value of land reflects the discounted income stream of future expected rents, transition to stewardship does not even take away from current owners their expectations of future increases in value. See Part V for a fuller description of transition.

Managing the environment

Efficiency

In an ownership economy....

It is helpful to distinguish between four types of property. The difference between them is: 'who has the power to exclude others from it and to decide how it is used?'

Private property, where an individual or other legal entity decides.

Collective property, where the decision is made by reference to the collective interest of society as a whole.

Common property, where the members of a defined community decide.

Open access regimes, where all are free to use the resource as they want.

Many aspects of the environment have, until very recently, been managed as open access regimes, common property or collective property. Although village-level common property has a long history of generally successful environmental management, collective property has often been badly managed and open access regimes have led to over-use, pollution and exploitation. One reason for these problems is that those who use the environment have no financial incentive to take into account the impact they have on it.

The traditional responses to environmental problems have been regulation and legislation, but economists and governments have increasingly turned to private property rights and the price mechanism to shape the behaviour of both consumers and producers.

True cost pricing. One way of ensuring that prices reflect the true cost, including costs to society and the environment, is to tax damaging activities. Another way is to establish tradable property rights in that aspect of the environment.

In a stewardship economy….

Stewardship makes it possible to manage the environment by providing a well-designed system of property rights.

Environment Stewardship Trusts.   Each aspect of the environment is held in trust by an Environment Stewardship Trust. The Trust may use a variety of approaches to manage its aspect of the environment including regulation, subsidies and promoting legislation and taxation.   But it is likely to favour auctioning tradable permits.

Enforcement. This approach only works if the Trust is able to enforce the surrender of permits whenever the environment is used and to prevent unauthorised use.

Private property rights. A permit to emit, extract or access the environment for a defined length of time is a form of private property right.

Making the best use of the environment. The auction of permits ensures that the environment is used by those who value it most highly and should therefore make best use of it.

A market in permits. The first market in permits is the auction at which they are allocated by the Environment Stewardship Trust. As the permits are tradable, secondary markets will arise.   A futures market establishes anticipated future prices and allows hedging against price fluctuations, though this brings with it the danger of speculation.

True cost pricing. The price that firms and individuals pay for environmental permits provides an incentive to make the most efficient use of environmental resources. As the cost is passed on to consumers, goods and services are sold at a price that reflects their true cost including their cost to the environment and to society. True cost pricing provides consumers with a financial incentive to reduce consumption and find a path to sustainable development.

Managing the environment

Fairness

In an ownership economy....

Private property rights may be an efficient way to manage the environment, but there is no guarantee that they are fair. When the essentials of life, like water, are taken into private ownership this provokes an understandable outcry. Open access regimes may be inefficient, but at least they are fair.

When private property rights and prices that reflect true costs are introduced, much of the sense of fairness or unfairness depends on whether poor people are able to afford the essentials of life. People are unforgiving when the value of the natural resources in question (the resource rent) is appropriated either as corporate profits or as a 'stealth tax'.

When private property rights are introduced, they are often gifted to organisations whose support the government needs. One of the best-known examples of tradable emissions permits is the regime of carbon permits, under the European Emissions Trading Scheme, which large producers have to surrender when they emit carbon dioxide. In the early years of the scheme these private property rights to greenhouse gas emissions have been gifted to the major polluters ('grandfathering') – and lobbying by these polluters resulted in the gift of extra allocations of permits that undermined the viability of the entire scheme.

The European Union has rewarded the 'first occupants' who have polluted the atmosphere without having to pay the cost. Fortunately, these permits are not gifts in perpetuity but are limited in duration; and the British government favours auctioning an increasing proportion of the permits.

A separate issue is that the price increases that environmental charges, such as tradable permits, are designed to bring about are unfair in an ownership economy in which wealth is so unequally distributed.

In a stewardship economy....

From the perspective of efficiency, it does not matter how permits are distributed as long as they can be traded. But a fundamental principle of stewardship is that each person has the right to an equal share of the wealth of the natural world. The idea that a claim of first occupancy or first use could justify private ownership is even less plausible for the environment than it is for land.

Auctioning permits. In an established stewardship economy firms buy permits at auction rather than acquiring them by grandfathering. This puts all polluters on an equal footing, rather than subsidising established polluters.

Renewable resources. Permit auctions establish the market rent of these natural resources, which is paid into a fund, the *whole* of which is distributed as an Environmental Dividend. This means that somebody who uses a fair (equal) share of those resources neither gains nor loses. Those who use more than their fair share compensate those who use less. This has exactly the same effect as rationing, provided that rations are legally tradable rather than restricted for personal use. This arrangement makes environmental charges much fairer than they are in ownership economies.

Non-renewable resources. A stewardship economy auctions permits for extracting non-renewable resources in a similar way. Fairness to future generations requires that our activities do not compromise their opportunities, which means that the revenue (resource rent) obtained from the extraction of non-renewable resources should be re-invested for the benefit of future generations. Ideally, the revenue from the auction of these permits should not be distributed as an Environmental Dividend but invested, particularly to produce substitutes for the resources that are being depleted.

Raising revenue

Efficiency

In an ownership economy....

Distortions introduced by taxes. Conventional taxes – whether they fall on labour, alcohol, value added or windows – are inefficient in the sense that that they diminish whatever they are levied on: work, drinking, adding value or natural lighting, for example. Taxes distort the allocation of resources – for example taxes on labour discourage labour-intensive activities and so employment, and taxes on capital discourage investment in capital-intensive activities.

Deadweight loss. Even more importantly it is widely recognised in orthodox economics that taxes on income, profits, value added and so on cause a reduction in economic activity and growth that is known as the deadweight loss. A conservative estimate of the deadweight loss of all taxes in the UK is around £100 billion per year, eight per cent of GDP. The firms made unprofitable by these taxes are those on the least productive sites, in the most deprived areas.

Inefficiencies of collection. Tax collection is also inefficient – a proportion of each tax is lost as a result of:

o avoidance and evasion

o uncertainties and ambiguities, for example which country a tax falls due in

o costs of collecting each tax.

In a global economy, corporations can relocate to take advantage of low-tax regimes and rich individuals can move to tax havens. National governments have to compete to provide an economic environment that is attractive to businesses by lowering taxes on capital and on mobile workers. Increasingly they will be driven to put more tax on immobile factors like unskilled workers and consumption – or, more optimistically, on land.

In a stewardship economy....

No distortion introduced by taxes. Stewardship fees are different from conventional taxes because they don't reduce the amount of land or the environment that is made available. Indeed, they act as a stimulus to the economy by making land available.

No deadweight loss. Taxes on things like land that are fixed in supply, known as Ramsey taxes, are economically efficient in that they do not reduce overall economic activity – they impose no deadweight loss. This key feature of stewardship is displayed graphically elsewhere.

A stewardship economy therefore functions rather as a tax haven does in an ownership world – it attracts individuals and corporations that flourish in an environment where there are no taxes. All firms benefit, including those that can use the least productive sites, and this promotes economic growth and employment in deprived areas.

Efficiency of collection. Stewardship fees are almost impossible to avoid or evade as land can't be hidden or moved abroad. There is no hidden economy in which work is done without taxes being paid. Stewards have a powerful incentive to pay the fee for their land, as it is this payment that establishes their title.

Stewardship fees are no cheaper to collect than any other form of taxation; indeed, they may be more expensive to collect than some other forms of tax. But as a single source of revenue the stewardship fee would cost far less to collect than a portfolio of dozens of forms of tax.

An important aspect of stewardship fees for land is that (unlike environmental charges) they cannot be passed on to tenants and consumers. This has been uncontroversial amongst orthodox economists since Adam Smith.

Raising revenue

Fairness

In an ownership economy....

The purpose of a tax is to provide revenue for the state. All taxes take away from people, or firms, part of something that is theirs.

The usual criteria for judging the fairness of taxes are the 'ability to pay' principle and the 'benefit principle'. Both can be recognised in Adam Smith's first maxim of taxation. There are two other criteria that are at least as important – non-confiscation and positive effects.

Non-confiscation. A tax should ideally not fall on something that somebody rightly owns, such as their labour.

Positive effects. Taxes may have positive effects. Taxes on tobacco and alcohol reduce the burden of ill-health, and environmental taxes reduce environmental damage. Taxes should be judged by their ability to do good as well as to do least harm.

Ability to pay. The 'ability to pay' principle may be interpreted as advocating payment in proportion to total income, or to what can be spared once the necessities of life have been provided, or even to total wealth.

Benefit. The benefit principle suggests that taxes should fall on taxpayers 'in proportion... to the revenue which they respectively enjoy under the state' (Adam Smith 1776: Volume III Book V Chapter II: 208). This is usually interpreted either as a tax in proportion to total income or in proportion to the goods and services provided by the state.

Orthodox economists recognise that all conventional taxes, even though they may be necessary, are fundamentally unfair as well as inefficient. Most recommend a combination of taxes so that their impact is not borne excessively by any one group of taxpayers.

In a stewardship economy….

Non-confiscation. Stewardship fees are fees or charges (paid to secure a particular benefit), not taxes (paid to raise revenue for the state). This may seem like a semantic quibble, but stewardship fees do not support the state by taking away from people something that is rightly theirs – such as their labour, the return on their capital, the value they add, their profits. Stewardship fees are the by-products of the fairest imaginable way to allocate land, namely, payment of its market rent.

Positive effect. Stewardship fees stimulate the best land use.

Ability to pay. Landlords, and firms that own their own properties, are able to pay their stewardship fees as long as the land is being put to good commercial use.

The same is not true for all owner-occupiers. A poorer person who lives in a high-value property faces a stewardship fee that is not affordable. They could decide to move to a smaller property or to a less desirable area; but this may be very hard, particularly if they have lived there for a long time. This situation needs to be handled sensitively with special measures to enable them to stay in their home if they want to.

Benefit. The market rent of a site arises because desirable locations are scarce, which creates competition for that site. Its value depends on the sum of all its desirable features –fitness for use, transport connections, availability of skilled labour, security, infrastructure support, good schools and so on. This location value, created by the community, is assessed as its market rent and returned to the community. Nothing could be closer to the benefit principle.

Transition. Rapid introduction of full stewardship fees into an ownership economy would amount to immediate confiscation of the value of the land and could not be justified. A fairer approach is discussed in Part V.

Benefit systems

Efficiency

In an ownership economy....

The purpose of a benefit system in an ownership economy is to provide the greatest relief from poverty and suffering that can be achieved with a limited amount of revenue.

An efficient benefit system delivers the greatest possible proportion of the available resource to its intended recipients.

Eligibility. Benefits are generally targeted at those who benefit most, which means that most benefits are conditional on meeting some criterion such as poverty or unemployment. National Insurance benefits are conditional on the recipient's contribution record.

Work, study and re-training. The critical flaw in conditional benefit systems is that they create a barrier that prevents people from taking up work, particularly low-paid and part-time work – the unemployment and poverty traps. They also deter people from making the transition back to full health.

Savings. Benefits that are conditional on poverty may discourage people from saving.

Take-up. National Assistance benefits are conditional on means-testing and have a poor take-up – for example the over-60s fail to claim £5 billion in means-tested benefits each year. The take-up of unconditional benefits like Basic State Pension and Child Benefit is, by contrast, high.

Cost of delivering benefit. The cost of delivering benefits varies considerably – Child Benefit, an unconditional and universal benefit, costs just over 1 per cent of the benefit delivered while unemployment benefit costs 21 per cent.

Benefit fraud. About 2 per cent of benefits are estimated to be lost through fraud.

In a stewardship economy….

The intention of the Universal Income is to distribute to the whole population their share of the wealth of the land.

Eligibility. The Universal Income is entirely unconditional and is unrelated to poverty, income, wealth, past history of work, present work status and availability for work, family unit, marital status, gender or ethnicity. The amount paid may, or may not, be related to age. There is no means test.

Work, study, re-training and volunteering. The Universal Income is paid whether or not the recipient is working or volunteering. There is no withdrawal of benefit when they start to work, whether this is full-time or part-time, and so there is no disincentive to work.

Universal Income also provides income for people who are studying or re-training to prepare themselves for work, and income to support them when volunteering.

Self-reliance and saving. The Universal Income is unconditional and so is not withdrawn from people who have savings. This means that people are more likely to take responsibility for their own future and to save, including making provision for a private pension.

Take-up. It is reasonable to anticipate that take-up of the Universal Income would approach 100 per cent.

Cost of delivering benefit is likely to be less than for Child Benefit as the costs per recipient are similar while the amount of benefit paid may be significantly higher.

Benefit fraud. Universal Income would not be free from fraud, but it would be much more straightforward to prevent excessive or duplicate claims where the benefit is genuinely universal.

Benefit systems

Fairness

In an ownership economy....

Child Benefit, which is unconditional, has had quite a wide base of popular support as it is fair and transparent – as well as binding the middle classes into the benefit system. Economists dislike universal unconditional benefits because the taxes required to fund them cause a deadweight loss, and this makes them an easy target for a cost-cutting government. Most other benefits are conditional, and these are unfair to recipients in a number of ways:

Poverty. Benefit levels are too low to live a rewarding life.

Tests of conditionality, such as means tests and tests of disability, may be humiliating as well as reducing take-up.

People who have been out of paid work – for example carers of parents and children – are disadvantaged and treated as though their contribution to society has been less important than those in employment.

Women often receive lower levels of benefit than men – their National Insurance record is often incomplete because they have taken those caring roles.

Household assessment. Allocating benefits to households rather than to individuals is unavoidable when benefits are conditional on poverty, but this may penalise someone who shares accommodation with others. This is not just unfriendly to families but to a variety of co-ownership and collective living arrangements. It also encourages the agency paying benefits to inquire into the living arrangements of claimants, for example whether a couple co-habits.

Judgements. Conditional benefits are corrupting to taxpayers who are seduced into making moral judgements about 'worthiness' or 'unworthiness' of the recipients.

In a stewardship economy....

Recipients and taxpayers recognise Universal Income to be fair provided that they accept that stewardship is a fair property system. Universal Income supports even those without access to land. It is fair, supportive, non-intrusive, non-judgemental and respectful of differences between people. It meets a very fundamental notion of fairness, even though it is not tailored to individual need.

Universal Income is intended to take the place of several traditional benefits including Child Benefit, Basic State Pension and Tax Credits. It is not the only benefit paid in a stewardship economy – additional payments are paid in socialist and liberal versions of stewardship to people with additional needs, particularly to people with sickness and disability and to carers. There are a variety of possible ways to implement Universal Income during transition.

Poverty. Universal Income provides a small independent income that is not withdrawn and can be used as a platform on which to assemble other forms of income, including part-time and low-paid work.

Tests of conditionality. Nobody has to demonstrate their poverty and there is no means testing with its associated humiliations and poor uptake.

People who have been out of paid work are treated the same as those who have been in work.

Women receive the same income as men.

Household assessment. Payments are to individuals, who can choose whether to share accommodation with others.

Judgements. Universal Income liberates taxpayers from the self-destructive habit of making value judgements about other people's lives.

Challenges as well as opportunities

From a range of perspectives, a stewardship economy poses significant challenges as well as having a great deal to offer:

- ❏ Right-libertarians find it in conflict with their belief that the first occupant of land and natural resources has the right to claim private ownership rights in perpetuity on the basis of historical entitlement. Left libertarians, by contrast, advocate equal rights to the wealth of the natural world. All libertarians support the removal of taxes on income and enterprise.

- ❏ Socialists may distrust stewardship's private property rights and market mechanisms – even though many would support an unconditional Universal Income.

- ❏ Greens, very understandably, fear that making the economy work more efficiently would result in unrestrained growth. Some feel that the natural world and private property, even in the form of stewardship, are incompatible (Stuart McBurney 1990: 53) and that using financial instruments to manage the natural world is morally wrong. The Green party does, however, embrace both Land Value Taxation and Citizen's Income.

- ❏ Most people are challenged by the suggestion that we all have a right to a share of the common wealth, whatever our involvement in paid work – even though they can see that conditional benefits are demeaning, fail to reach those who really need them and discourage work and savings.

- ❏ Most people in the UK have invested their financial security so profoundly in the expected rise in the price of their home that they cannot countenance the stable land prices of a stewardship economy – even though they would receive a Universal Income that rises as the market rent of land rises across the country.

In summary: The claim that a stewardship economy is *fair* stems from the assertion that, in an ideal world, stewardship is a fair form of private property – for land and the environment. Ownership of artefacts is unchanged in a stewardship economy.

A steward acquires the use of land or the environment, not as a result of an historical entitlement but because of a current willingness to pay regular compensation to all those who are excluded from using it.

These payments provide the basis for a fair way to raise revenue. While conventional taxes take from people and firms a proportion of the wealth on which they have a legitimate claim, stewardship collects location values that are created by the community. And a Universal Income is fairer than conditional benefits, provided that the revenue to fund it is obtained fairly.

Stewardship is also more *efficient* than conventional systems of taxation as it does not distort the economy or impose a deadweight loss. Universal Income is an efficient form of benefit, as it does not discourage people from working, has a high take-up and is relatively free from fraud.

Stewardship provides a fair and efficient way to manage the environment that confronts consumers and producers with prices that reflect the true cost of their activities. This is fair, because the distribution of the Environmental Dividend ensures that those who use less than their equal share are net beneficiaries

Chapter 13 How to make it work

This chapter describes how the challenges of valuing land for stewardship differ from those in an ownership economy (for example, for Land Value Taxation). It then outlines the practicalities of valuation and collection of stewardship fees. It provides a summary of material that is presented at greater depth in Book 2, which contains more detailed explanations, evidence and references.

Remember that this is a description of a mature steady state stewardship economy – transition from an ownership economy is described in Chapter 14.

Valuation in an ownership economy

Valuation by market transaction

The 'gold standard' for assessing either the market value or the market rent of land is to offer the land in a market in which there are a number of knowledgeable and prudent bidders.

Valuation by comparison

The next-best alternative is the opinion of a well-informed and expert valuer. The most common basis of valuation is valuation by comparison. Here the land in question is compared with other plots of land that have changed hands on the open market in the recent past. The expertise of the valuer includes their ability to identify true 'comparables' and to make allowances for differences between the comparables and the property to be valued.

Impact of Land Value Taxation on the land market

100 per cent of market rent

If a perfect valuer could accurately assess the market rent of all properties in an ownership economy, and if Land Value Taxation was then introduced at 100 per cent of the market rent, the market rent *net of Land Value Tax* of all land would fall to zero; as would the market value of the land.

Critics of Land Value Taxation often assume that the tax is assessed as a proportion either of the market value of land or of the net market rent, and therefore that Land Value Taxation erodes its own tax base. The simple response to this is that a Land Value Tax is assessed as a proportion of the gross market rent (net market rent plus Land Value Tax). But putting this into practice in the current land market is not so simple.

Advocates of Land Value Taxation generally propose that, just as a valuer could produce accurate valuations in the absence of Land Value Taxation, once the tax has been introduced all the valuer has to do is to adjust their valuations up and down according to the local economic climate. They could fine-tune their valuations by reducing the level of Land Value Tax if they found that unimproved land was left unoccupied or if improved land was changing hands for less than the value of the improvements; and by increasing the level of Land Value Tax if unimproved land changed hands for a significant market value or improved land sold for a premium over the value of the improvements.

This leaves open the question of how properties would be transferred from one owner to the next. In the case of unimproved land, the owner could expect to put the property on the market and sell it for a peppercorn. In the case of improved land, they would sell it to whoever was prepared to pay the value of the improvements. This is clearly a long way from the sort of land market that we are familiar with today.

Up to 100 per cent of market rent

There have been no problems when Land Value Taxation has been introduced in ownership economies, as the tax has been levied at no more than 10-20 per cent of the market rent of land, equivalent to about 0.5-1.0 per cent of its market (sale) value. At this level of taxation, the market value of land is not greatly reduced, and the tax does not interfere with the assessment of tax liabilities. There is plenty of experience of assessing land values in ownership economies with this level of Land Value Taxation.

Even if a tax were to be levied at 50 per cent of the market rent of land, assessment of tax liabilities would still be possible. In an ownership economy with no Land Value Taxation a plot of land with a market rent of £5,000 per year would have a market value in the region of £100,000. If half of this (gross) market rent were to be collected as tax, then the tax of £2,500 would be equal to the net market rent paid to the owner. The market value would fall to around £50,000, and the tax would amount to 5 per cent of the market value. The level of tax would be sensitive to errors in the valuation, but not unduly so.

If the tax were to be levied at 90 per cent of (gross) market rent it would amount to £4,500 per year. The market value of the plot would be reduced to just £10,000 and the annual tax would amount to 45 per cent of this, or nine times the net market rent. A small error in this market value (or market rent) would have a big impact on the amount of tax to be paid and valuations would be likely to be contested. In addition, a buyer would be deciding how much to offer on the basis of the ongoing liability of £4,500 per year rather than the one-off purchase price of £10,000.

I suggest that, if a Land Value Tax were collected at over 50 per cent of market rent, there would need to be a new sort of land market in which everybody acquiring property bid the market rent and not the market value.

The new land market in a stewardship economy

Unimproved land

The simplest challenge for this new land market is the transfer of
land that has no buildings or other improvements on it –
unimproved land. The most transparent way in which this transfer
can take place in the market is by means of a public auction in
which the plot of land is transferred to the stewardship of the bidder
who is prepared to pledge to pay the highest annual stewardship
fee. The level of the fee is thus established by the auction. This
provides a fair, transparent and simple way to discover the market
rent of land at the time of transfer.

The market value of unimproved land is zero and the outgoing
steward will not receive any payment from the transaction. The
potential problem is that the outgoing steward has no financial
incentive to seek the highest bid and so to establish the market rent
of the site.

For this reason, in a stewardship economy all land transactions
must take place in an independent auction conducted by the Land
Stewardship Trust, not by direct contract between buyer and seller.

I use the term 'new land market' to describe this market in
which all transfers are made through auctions conducted by the
Land Stewardship Trust and all bids are for annual payments of the
market rent.

Buildings and other improvements

What usually comes to market is not unimproved land but
properties that comprise both land and buildings. How could we
value these independently of each other? A single market
transaction can put a value on the whole, but not on land and
improvements independently of each other.

It is possible to value a new building without exposing the
whole property to the market – indeed this is one of the things a
quantity surveyor will do for any proposed new building at the time
of its design. The task is first to translate the architectural drawings

into a 'bill of quantities' that lists all the components and materials from which the building is constructed. From this the total price of the materials can be estimated. Quantity surveyors can also estimate how much time, for each type of building worker, will be needed for the construction. In this way they can estimate the total cost of the new building.

When the construction work is put out to tender, the quantity surveyor's estimate is tested in the market against the similar calculations made by each of the contractors. It is the tender that is accepted that determines the building cost.

When the building has just been completed, this cost of construction is, by definition, the building's 'replacement cost'. As the building ages, its value falls as a result of deterioration and obsolescence to a value described as its 'Depreciated Replacement Cost'. In principle the value of a building can be established independently of the market for land, provided that the extent of depreciation can be established.

The value of land, on the other hand, cannot be established with confidence without either exposing it to the market or comparing it with a similar plot (a comparable) that has itself been exposed. The only alternative would be for the valuer to think themself into the heads of all the people who might want to acquire the stewardship of the site, imagine how they might use it and what benefit they might get from it, estimate how much income it might generate and how much rent each could offer to pay. Clearly this is a highly subjective and uncertain approach.

For this reason, the Land Stewardship Trust's preferred approach is to value buildings and other improvements by asking a professional valuer to estimate the improvement value as a Depreciated Replacement Cost; and to value land by exposing it to the market.

Improved land

If the property in question includes buildings or other improvements as well as land, the new land market requires that all transfers be made through auctions conducted by the Land Stewardship Trust and that all bids be for annual payments of the market rent. A potential purchaser has to pledge, as a pre-condition of entry to the auction, to pay the value of the buildings (the 'improvement value') to the seller if the bid is successful. The auction then proceeds as before, with stewardship allocated to whoever bids the highest stewardship fee.

Valuing the improvements

Clearly the stewardship fee that an incoming steward will offer depends on the price that is put on the improvements. Establishing this improvement value as a Depreciated Replacement Cost is a skilled job and the valuation may be contested. These issues are discussed in detail elsewhere, along with all aspects of valuation, depreciation and the new land market.

Keeping valuations up to date

Annual review

To keep the valuation up to date, without requiring an annual auction, a professional valuer makes an annual assessment of the market rent. They do so by comparing it with similar plots that have been sold at auction during the previous year – comparables. These comparisons are facilitated by the use of computer-based geographic information systems (GIS) that contain information about all local property transactions.

Appeal

If a steward thinks that the assessment of the market rent is incorrect, or that land values have fallen since the last assessment, they can at any time ask for the property to be put to auction. They can then bid a lower stewardship fee and will retain stewardship if this is the highest bid received.

Collecting stewardship fees

Collecting stewardship fees is no more difficult than collecting Income Tax or VAT, and far more straightforward than collecting a bundle of conventional taxes. Each steward has a strong incentive to pay on time, as they have to pay the stewardship fee to retain their title to the land.

What this means for home ownership

It may help to bring this description of the new land market to life to describe what this means for buying and selling a home.

The first step in acquiring a home in an established stewardship economy, as in an ownership economy, is to identify the home. You might go to an intermediary, such as a relocation agent or an estate agent, whom you can trust to find the sort of property you want; or you might search independently. An independent search is easier than in an ownership economy because all the properties that are currently available are listed in the local databases managed by the Land Stewardship Trust. The information available to you includes the cost of both elements of the property – the purchase price for the building and other improvements (the improvement value) and the current stewardship fee for the land.

After you have chosen the property that you want to acquire, you enter an auction. The necessary pre-conditions such as legal searches and identifying a source of finance are the same in a stewardship economy as they are for auction sales in an ownership economy. The auction itself might take the same form as an Internet auction on eBay, and, if you are successful, you are committed to buy at the moment the auction closes.

As you bid, you are committing yourself to do two things. The first is to pay the improvement value to the seller of the property; the second is to pay whatever level of stewardship fee you are bidding. This annual fee is payable to the Land Stewardship Trust in monthly instalments. The current stewardship fee should be a guide to what you need to bid, but it might not be – what you have to do is to outbid your competitors.

So, you win the auction, pay the improvement value to the outgoing steward and start your monthly payments of the stewardship fee. You now own the buildings and other improvements and are steward of the land. You are as free to alter and develop your property as you are in an ownership economy. If you do something that increases the value of the buildings, you can apply to the Land Stewardship Trust to have the improvement value increased. This will ensure that you recoup your investment when you sell the property. Your monthly outgoings are probably pretty similar to those in an ownership economy and are made up of the mortgage payments (interest and capital repayments) for the building plus the stewardship fee for the land. Your level of debt is less than it would be in an ownership economy because you have only had to take out a mortgage on the buildings, not the land.

Over the course of time, the value of your property will change. The value of the buildings will rise if you undertake new building and fall as the buildings deteriorate. Just as in an ownership economy, the general trend of the market rent of the land tends to be upwards but there are times when it could fall; either for national reasons (such as a recession) or for local reasons (such as unfavourable local developments).

Each year, on the anniversary of your purchase, the Land Stewardship Trust uses evidence of the stewardship fees of comparables that have been exposed to the market to adjust the stewardship fee.

For as long as you pay the stewardship fee, you have security of tenure. If you think that the stewardship fee is too high, you can appeal to the market.

Over the years, as stewardship fees tend to rise, you will find that your monthly outgoings increase. This is what tenants, but not owner-occupiers, experience in an ownership economy. Stewardship fees reflect the value of your land now, not at the time you bought it. But there is a compensation – in a stewardship economy you receive a Universal Income, which also increases over the years as stewardship fees rise around the country. In an established stewardship economy, the increase in your Universal Income would reimburse you for the increase in your stewardship fee provided that your home represents an equal per capita share of the value of all the land in the country (including industrial, commercial and agricultural land as well as housing land). If the land your household occupies is smaller or less desirable than average for that size of household, you will be a net gainer from stewardship. If the land you occupy is larger or more desirable than average, you will be a net contributor.

When you want to sell the property, you ask the Land Stewardship Trust to put it up for auction and set a date. The Trust will pay to you, after the close of the auction, the improvement value. If you want to give or bequeath the property, you can do so by informing the Land Stewardship Trust which simply registers the change of steward (there are no transaction taxes like Stamp Duty Land Tax).

In a stewardship economy you will not think of your home as an investment that will automatically grow in value. Rather, you will think of it as you would a car or a caravan and expect that its value will fall in real (inflation-adjusted) terms. People in a stewardship economy derive their sense of financial security not from owning their own home but from their entitlement to the Universal Income.

In summary:

Stewardship needs a new land market, in which each property is transferred from steward to steward through the Land Stewardship Trust. This takes place by means of an auction, unless the transfer is by gift or bequest.

The new land market provides a practical way to establish the stewardship fee for a property, making use of market mechanisms, whenever a property changes hands. This provides a 'gold standard' valuation for that property and a valuable comparable for other properties.

The practical details of the new land market are described at greater length in Book 2.

PART V TRANSITION TO STEWARDSHIP

Chapter 14 Practicalities of transition

The principle that underlies these proposals for transition to a stewardship economy is that the owner retains the value of any property rights that exist at the onset of transition.

In this chapter I suggest how to make a transition to stewardship in three different circumstances:

- o transition of an environmental resource from an open access regime, common property or collective property – where there are no private property rights
- o transition from an ownership economy in which property rights to land are contested
- o transition from a legitimate ownership economy by setting the stewardship fee equal to the *increase* in market rent that occurs after the onset of transition to stewardship, thereby preserving the current property value for the owner.

Possibilities for transition are described at greater length in Book 2.

From open access regime or collective property

It is easiest to imagine how to make the transition from an ownership economy in the case of resources that are at present managed collectively, as an open access regime or as common property. The electromagnetic spectrum used to be managed as collective property but parts of it are now managed broadly as it would be in a stewardship economy. The atmospheric sink for greenhouse gases used to be managed as an open access regime but there is now a market in emissions permits for carbon dioxide and, as permits begin to be allocated by auction, this, too, is moving towards being managed in the way that it would be in a stewardship economy.

Satellite orbits have moved from an open access regime to a form of common property, with orbits allocated by agreement amongst the nations that use them. The use of the orbits for a defined length of time could be treated as private property and allocated by auction. The revenue from these resource rents could then be used to fund global interventions, as they would in a fully developed stewardship economy.

From a state with contested property rights

A different opportunity for transition occurs where current historically based claims to property rights to land are contested and people want to carry out land reform. From time to time, situations of this sort open up – for example there was a window of opportunity in Eastern Europe after the collapse of communism, and another might open in Zimbabwe after Robert Mugabe.

In such a case an immediate move to stewardship could provide a fair allocation of property rights to replace the prior, contested, rights.

Even the preparation for stewardship, in particular the establishment of a register of property rights, strengthens institutions and improves security of tenure.

From an established ownership economy

The greatest challenge – but also the greatest opportunity – is how to make the transition from a legitimate ownership economy. Most of those who have written in opposition to the introduction of Land Value Taxation have criticised not the ideal but its introduction into an ownership economy.

John Kenneth Galbraith, for example, agreed that if a Land Value Tax had been in place from the time that the United States was colonised it might have been considered fair, but that to introduce one now would discriminate against those who had bought land rather than those who had invested in railroads or steel mills (1987:168).

John Stuart Mill believed that it would be possible to make the transition to a tax on the rent of land without interfering with existing property rights by introducing a tax on any *future increase* in the market value of land that occurs after the introduction of the scheme:

> The present value of all land should be exempt from the tax; but after an interval had elapsed, during which society had increased in population and capital, a rough estimate might be made of the spontaneous increase which had accrued to rent since the valuation was made .... I see no objection to declaring that the future increment in rent should be liable to special taxation; in doing which every shadow of injustice to the landlords would be obviated, if the present market-price of their land were secured to them; since that includes the present value of all future expectations (1848 Book V Chapter 2 Section 5: 361-2).

This fully, and perhaps even excessively, provides for the owners' existing right to private property in land even while it denies their claim to future increases in its value. Mill's proposal was strongly opposed by Henry George, who wrote that 'it would leave, for all the future, one class in possession of the enormous advantage over others which they now have. All that can be said of this plan is, that it might be better than nothing.' (1879 Book VII Chapter III: 325). Perhaps now is the time to campaign for something that is better than nothing, for evolution rather than revolution.

The difference between Mill's "special taxation" and the transition to a mature stewardship economy is that eventually the "enormous advantage" of George's "one class in possession" of land will be eroded away, as increases in market rent eclipse their original value.

Principles of transition

The design for transition needs to be carried out carefully and in detail, with thorough modelling of the consequences – particularly how the changes affect people with different levels of income and wealth and living in different regions. Underlying this design there need to be a number of underlying principles:

Respect for existing property rights

The stewardship fee for a plot of land would be limited to the increase in its market rent after the onset of transition.

No penalties for the poorest

There must be a guarantee that none of the poorest and most disadvantaged members of society will be worse off at any stage of transition to stewardship.

No penalties for owners of low value homes

For homes of below-average market rent, there needs to be a guarantee that homeowners are better-off under stewardship than ownership.

How to do it

At the onset of transition, the Land Stewardship Trust assesses the value of each property – the price for which the land *together with* the buildings would change hands. This value, the 'Transitional Value', is used during transition in place of the Improvement Value (the Depreciated Replacement Cost of buildings and other replacements). If an owner is dissatisfied with this assessment of Transitional Value, they can appeal to the market.

Stewardship fees would be zero at the onset of transition. If a property were to be sold immediately after the onset of transition, the new steward would pay the Transitional Value to the seller and could acquire the property by bidding a stewardship fee of zero.

If this steward sold the property sometime later, they would recover the Transitional Value provided that land values had not fallen. If the market rent of the land had increased over the intervening time an incoming steward would need to bid, and pay, a stewardship fee.

If transition begins during a time of falling land values, there would be no stewardship fees to pay until land values rose above their level at the onset of transition. The course of transition depends critically on how depreciation of buildings is handled, and how allowance is made for the increase in the value of the buildings as building costs rise.

Please see book 2 for a fuller explanation of the vital issue of transition.

Using the revenue during transition

Transition is complicated, not because stewardship is complicated but because transition requires us to unravel the current system of taxes and benefits in a way that disadvantages as few people as possible, particularly the least well off.

As revenue becomes available from stewardship fees, it may be used in four ways:

- o   as a source of revenue to reduce the national debt
- o   to allow the removal of conventional taxes
- o   to introduce a Universal Income *in addition to* the existing benefit system.
- o   to introduce a Universal Income *as an alternative to* a set of existing benefits

Each of these options has some adverse consequences for the distribution of wealth. The development of a practical proposal for transition to stewardship would require a microsimulation exercise to explore each of these independently. It would then be possible to develop a hybrid option in which revenue is allocated between these four alternatives in a way that optimises the impact of transition on the distribution of wealth. Each of these options is discussed below:

To reduce the national debt

If transition took place in 'normal circumstances', there would be no question of using revenue from stewardship fees to fund government expenditure or to repay the national debt. If stewardship were used in this way it would correctly be recognised as a new tax, even if it operated in a more efficient way than conventional taxes.

But the government bailout of the failed financial system has transferred the problem of insolvency from the private sector to the state. John Lanchester (2010:190) gives us some grasp of the size of the problem when he points out that the cost to the US government was greater than the *total* cost of the Louisiana Purchase, the New Deal, the Marshall Plan, the entire budget of NASA including the moon landings, the 1980s Savings and Loan crisis and the wars in Korea, Vietnam and Iraq (all adjusted upwards for inflation). The current problem is how to tackle the resulting sovereign debt crisis in the context of recession followed by a period of low economic growth.

An obvious source of revenue is monetary reform. It was the failures in the banking system that precipitated the recession, and there is a rare public appetite for measures that recover something from the banks. If the nature of the subsidy that we grant to banks as a result of their monopoly right to create money as interest-bearing loans were more widely understood, there would surely be widespread support for the state to issue all money itself. This would remove from governments both the burden of interest payments and their dependence on the bond market.

The dominant political debate is, however, limited to the question of what government expenditure to cut; with only a minority arguing that this is the worst possible moment in the economic cycle to cut services and investment as this will increase many areas of government spending (benefits, health and social care) at the same time as reducing tax returns. Cuts and job losses will fall disproportionately on the poor and increase the levels of inequality.

The alternative to cuts is to increase taxes. Both tax increases and spending cuts cause immediate harm to the economy and risk pushing us back into recession, and there is an understandable difference of opinion as to which does more damage. But tax increases have the advantage that they are borne by the well-off as well as the poor. It is the well-off who have gained most from government expenditure to protect bank deposits and the wider financial system. It would be a lot fairer to ask them to contribute to the exchequer than to cut essential benefits and services. Indeed, there may be substantial popular support for the proposition that the people who should contribute most to balancing the government's books are those whose land values have been supported by the bailout of the financial system and who benefited from the housing bubble that caused the current crisis. Governments may find stewardship an attractive proposition in these circumstances.

The problem is that, by introducing stewardship as a tax (a source of government revenue) rather than as a charge, stewardship becomes just another stealth tax rather than a principled reform. This perception could be minimised if conventional taxes were first increased and then gradually replaced by stewardship fees. This would be a logical approach as the need for tax revenue is immediate while the revenue from stewardship fees becomes available only as the market rent of land rises.

To reduce existing taxes

Using the revenue to reduce existing taxes has obvious appeal for taxpayers, as this counterbalances the cost of stewardship fees for many people. It is fiscally neutral and can be carried out in a way that is transparent. It has the great advantage of stimulating the economy by removing the deadweight loss of conventional taxes.

If transition for domestic and non-domestic properties were handled separately, both businesses and householders would see that the collection of stewardship fees is counterbalanced by a fall in conventional taxes. A start could be made with non-domestic properties, as businesses would immediately feel a direct benefit and there would be no opposition from homeowners.

The fairest approach would be to begin by using the revenue to remove taxes that currently fall on property, and then to move on to regressive taxes that fall on the poor. So, the revenue from commercial properties could be used to reduce the Non-Domestic (Business) Rates then Stamp Duty Land Tax, National Insurance contributions, VAT and eventually Corporation Tax. Revenue from stewardship fees on people's homes could be used to reduce Council Tax, then Stamp Duty Land Tax, VAT and eventually Income Tax.

The main problem with this use of the revenue is that there is a group of homeowners, often retired, who have low levels of income and pay relatively little tax at present but who would face significant stewardship fees.

Universal Income as an addition

In an economy where there are virtually no existing benefits the introduction of Universal Income is relatively simple – in a pilot in Namibia the distribution of $12 per person per month has, within a year, increased economic activity and cut undernutrition (Malcolm Torry 2009:1).

If Universal Income were to be introduced *in addition to* the extensive system of benefits found in most high-consumption economies, it would benefit everybody without disrupting the current system. The problem with this approach is that it offers no opportunity, even in the long run, of reforming the existing conditional benefit system with all of its disadvantages.

Universal Income as an alternative

The challenges of introducing a Universal Income as an alternative to a set of existing benefits mirrors the complexity of a mature ownership economy. Some benefits, such as those paid to people with disabilities and with caring responsibilities, would be retained in any liberal or socialist stewardship economy, as would sickness benefit. But there are several sorts of benefit that should be replaced in a stewardship economy. One group, the replacement of which is no more than a simplification of the benefit system, are those that are close to being universal for a particular age group (Child Benefit and Basic State Pension). Another group of payments that should be replaced by Universal Income are Tax Credits for those on low income and benefits for those who are out of work. A Universal Income offers the prospect of raising people out of dependence on these conditional benefits.

The problem with introducing Universal Income as an alternative is that the existing benefit system is closely designed to meet people's needs. If these benefits were withdrawn pound for pound as the Universal Income is introduced, the poor (those on benefits in an ownership economy) would be the last to benefit from transition to stewardship.

Hybrid options

There are many possible ways to remove taxes and introduce Universal Income, each with a different impact on the distribution of wealth and income. It will be critically important to explore and model in advance the impact on a range of different people before making a choice of approach.

One example of a hybrid worth exploring would be:

o benefits for people with disabilities and people with caring responsibilities are retained in full

o a proportion of all stewardship fees is used to replace taxes introduced to reduce the national debt

o the rest of the revenue from land that is used for business purposes (commercial, industrial, retail and agricultural) is used to replace taxes on business

o the rest of the revenue from residential land is used to introduce a Universal Income

o the Universal Income is treated as taxable income until Income Tax is removed o for every £1 per week of Universal Income a person's existing benefit package would be reduced by around 20p - 40p per week.

The intent behind this package is that it would contribute to reducing the national debt, benefit business by removing existing taxes on business and provide additional income for people on low income while gradually phasing out existing benefits. The detail would need to be carefully modelled and compared with other possible hybrid options.

In summary: This chapter has outlined some of the opportunities and challenges for transition, including a set of principles that should underpin detailed planning.

Transition to stewardship will take place over a long timescale, probably decades. It requires detailed modelling to ensure that the balance of costs and benefits falls fairly on all, and that the poorest are protected from any reduction in their disposable income

PART VI OPPORTUNITIES AND CHALLENGES

This final part of the book looks at what we might do with the possibilities suggested so far.

Chapter 15 explores the political realities of introducing stewardship into an ownership economy.

Chapter 16 sets out some of the areas that need further research and refers to individuals and organisations that are developing the thinking about the ideas that underlie stewardship.

Chapter 15 The political challenge

I have taken no account so far of the politics of making a transition from ownership to stewardship, other than to acknowledge that it will be difficult. The politics are only worth considering if you are convinced that the sort of economy described above in Part III is desirable, that the ethical and pragmatic justifications described in Chapter 12 are convincing and that the practical arrangements described in Chapters 13 & 14 are workable.

The history of taxes on land has been one of reversals. The expectation that land taxes will be reversed bolsters opponents of stewardship. The transition I propose would be a gradual one, so it would require a broad and deep political consensus that goes beyond an agreement that stewardship would be a 'good idea'.

This chapter does not lay out a political programme for making a transition to stewardship, but it does identify some of those who benefit from either ownership or stewardship. Those who benefit from stewardship may be expected to be broadly supportive and those who are better-off under ownership to be fiercely antagonistic, so it is important to model the detail of the transition to stewardship so that the detail of the proposal ensures that there are as few people as possible who would be better-off in an ownership economy. We cannot expect people to vote for anything that sounds like 'more taxes'. Proposals for a 'tax shift' from taxes on enterprise and income to 'smart taxes' on land and the environment may have more support.

Resistance to stewardship

The property requirement for voters for elections to the House of Commons was not lifted until the Representation of the People Act of 1918. The House of Lords was, until only a few years ago, made up largely of the great landowners. Not surprisingly landowners supported measure after measure to reduce their responsibility for contributing to state revenue.

John Kenneth Galbraith has argued persuasively in *The Culture of Contentment* (1992:15) that, in a high-consumption economy, a majority of those who vote are the contented beneficiaries of the status quo; so, there is no majority support for tax rises that would benefit the poor and disadvantaged.

The proportion of households that own their own primary residence, the home ownership rate, is around 70 per cent in the UK. Homeowners generally oppose stewardship because they will no longer benefit from any future increase in house prices – even though they would benefit from a Universal Income, reduction in or freedom from other taxes and a buoyant and inclusive economy. 'A social process exists that now survives by co-opting people into exploiting themselves.' (Fred Harrison 2006b: 9).

Steven Lukes has argued that power is not limited to the making of decisions on issues over which there is an observable conflict of interests (decisions - the first dimension of power); or to the prevention of decisions being taken on potential issues over which there is an observable conflict of interests (controlling the agenda – the second dimension of power).

The third dimension of power is the power to prevent people from having grievances by shaping their perceptions and preferences in such a way that they accept their role in the existing order of things – a view that he acknowledges to be inspired by Antonio Gramsci's notion of ideological hegemony. This third dimension of power keeps out of the political arena those potential issues where there is a latent conflict between the interests of those exercising power and the real interests of those they exclude (1974:24). It ensures the consent of the excluded without conflict being apparent. Those of us who question the validity of ownership of the natural world have not been defeated (first dimension) or prevented from discussing the issue (second dimension), but it does not feature on the political radar or in the consciousness of most broadsheet readers.

It may be that the explanation for the widespread resistance to stewardship is even simpler than this. Perhaps we are just locked into the institution of private ownership in the same way that we are locked in to the technology of the QWERTY keyboard – an initially useful invention persists by historical accident, simply because we have invested so much in it, even though it may have become dysfunctional.

People who may be better-off with ownership

Owners of investment properties

Owners of investment properties are much better-off with ownership, where they benefit from the market rent, capital gains and low levels of tax, than they would be with stewardship. They would retain the value of their buildings, but the value of their land would fall to zero.

The impact on landlords is an intended feature of an established stewardship economy, and nothing needs to be done to mitigate it. During transition to stewardship, however, it is only the increase in market rent that is collected as the stewardship fee. Owners of investment properties lose none of the current value of their properties and have the opportunity either to develop a business model based solely on leasing their buildings or to divest themselves of unwanted properties.

Owner-occupiers

Local government, national government, firms, pension funds and individuals may all own the land that they use for business or residential purposes. In an ownership economy all of these are free from taxes on their land (apart from Council Tax and the Non-Domestic (Business) Rates) but would pay stewardship fees in a stewardship economy.

Individuals and firms with valuable property holdings would be better-off with ownership, as even the removal of Council Tax, Non-Domestic (Business) Rates, National Insurance, VAT and Corporation Tax would not compensate them for their liability to pay stewardship fees. Those with less valuable holdings would be better-off with stewardship as they would gain more from the reduction or removal of conventional taxes than they would lose in stewardship fees. And everybody would be free from the anxiety of negative equity on their land.

Owner-occupiers on benefits

In ownership economies, low-income owner-occupiers are eligible for means-tested benefits because the market value of their home is disregarded when their eligibility for benefit is assessed. However, they do not receive housing benefit, as this is only available to people who pay rent.

In a stewardship economy all owner-occupiers are liable to pay stewardship fees. If the revenue from stewardship fees is used to reduce conventional taxes this may be enough to compensate those in work but is less help for those who are not working, including many pensioners. Without some targeted help, these owner-occupiers would be significantly better-off with ownership.

Owner-occupier stewards on low income will need additional financial support. One possibility would be to extend housing benefit during transition to include the payment of stewardship fees as well as rent. This could ensure that this group were no worse off with stewardship.

Owner-occupiers living alone

The cost of housing for one person is more than half the cost of an equivalent home shared between two people. This is of little consequence in an ownership economy for owner-occupiers who have paid off their mortgage, as their housing costs are low, but in a stewardship economy a steward living alone faces a much higher stewardship fee than two or more people sharing a home.

Similar issues arise in the benefit system – a single pensioner in an ownership economy receives a Pension Credit of about a third more than that received by each member of a pensioner couple, while they receive no additional income in a stewardship economy.

Stewardship favours those who make the most efficient use of land by downsizing to a home with fewer bedrooms or by sharing a home. It is possible that over a long time-scale it might promote more co-habitation, co-ownership and communal living.

Charities

Charities are subsidised in ownership economies by exemption from many forms of taxation. In a stewardship economy they would have to pay stewardship fees for their land, just like any other steward. This has important implications, particularly for those whose purpose is to hold land in trust like the National Trust, the Royal Society for the Protection of Birds and Community Land Trusts.

It is essential that, in a stewardship economy, charities are fully supported by a planning system that requires the steward of these lands to maintain and conserve them (or to provide social housing or whatever is the charitable aim). These requirements should be sufficient to keep stewardship fees down to low or even negative (subsidy) levels; but charities will also need a new stream of state subsidy to replace current tax exemptions.

People with more than their share of land

People and organisations with more than an equal share of land are better-off with ownership than they would be with stewardship. It's not difficult to imagine the uproar from the wealthy at any proposal to 'tax people for living in their own homes'. Indeed, just such a response forced the New Zealand government to repudiate the report of the McLeod committee which noted that 70 per cent of all savings in New Zealand is held in housing land and had recommended a tax on owner-occupied and rented housing.

Universal Income provides a way of sharing increases in market rent amongst the whole population, so those who have less than a fair (equal) share of land are better-off in a stewardship economy.

Transition is designed so that stewardship fees fall only on any increase in the market rent of land that occurs after the onset of transition, effectively phasing in the change gradually over what would probably be many decades and giving owners the choice of staying and paying or of moving to a property with a lower market rent.

Beneficiaries of state monopolies

Organisations that have been awarded a state monopoly in an ownership economy, for example radio spectrum, airport landing slots or a franchise to issue money as debt, are better-off in an ownership economy.

In a stewardship economy the organisation would make regular payments for the right to exercise this monopoly. This is the intended consequence of stewardship, and no mitigating measures would be taken – just a gradual transition.

Polluters

Polluters that have benefited from open access regimes or the grandfathering of permits are better-off in an ownership economy, though the days of passing the costs of pollution on to others are coming to an end even in ownership economies.

In a stewardship economy polluters will have to pay the cost of the pollution they cause. A polluter releasing average levels of pollution for that industry will be able to pass this cost on to consumers.

Tax and benefit experts

Many people with specialist expertise of the tax and benefit system may have an investment in the status quo, including accountants, tax advisors, benefits advisors, academics and civil servants.

During the period of transition, the skills of these people will be at a premium as there is a need for people who are expert in both the old ways and the new. A stewardship economy will continue to need these skills, focusing more on land and natural resources than in an ownership economy. The detail of the work that each of these groups carry out will be different in a stewardship economy but the transition provides the opportunity for acquiring new skills.

People who would be better-off with stewardship

People who support stewardship generally do so not out of self-interest but out of concern for the good of us all. It is, nevertheless, important to be aware of the groups who will benefit, as they may find it easier to hear about stewardship than people who are better-off with the status quo.

People with less than an equal share of land

Anybody who owns less than an equal share of land is a net beneficiary. This applies particularly to those who currently rent their home.

People who want access to land

Many people want access to land to put it to productive use, for example for small businesses, horticulture or small-scale agriculture. There is more land available in a stewardship economy, plot sizes are smaller, and there is no burden of raising financial capital to buy the land.

Businesses that rent their land.

Businesses that pay the market rent for the land they use in an ownership economy pay the same market rent in a stewardship economy but benefit from the reduction or absence of the Non-Domestic (Business) Rates, National Insurance contributions, VAT, Corporation Tax and so on.

People on benefits

In an established stewardship economy, people who would be on benefits in an ownership economy are better-off because they have the financial support of the Universal Income without any of the conditions, examinations and restrictions that are familiar in ownership economies. Their position during transition needs careful consideration.

People on low wages

People on low wages benefit from a small independent income, in the form of the Universal Income. They do not face the loss of their Universal Income if their earned income increases, so there is no poverty trap.

People who are looking for work

In a stewardship economy it is much easier to find work. There are more jobs, because the cost to employers is less – Income Tax and National Insurance contributions are reduced or cancelled. Jobs are more flexible, and part-time work is more attractive. Workers do not face an unemployment trap in which benefits are withdrawn when they start work.

Students

All students receive a Universal Income, which provides them with some financial support through their studies.

Surveyors, valuers and planners

Surveyors, valuers and planners will find that their professional skills are highly sought-after as the valuation and planning systems lie at the heart of business planning and the tax system.

Opportunities in the UK

Scotland

Tony Vickers (2007:11) has pointed out that charges on land values are particularly appropriate as the source of revenue for a devolved administration which needs to be able to raise revenue if it is to put its own policies into effect. Everybody who owns land in Scotland benefits from the investments made by the Scottish government, and a Land Value Tax would enable them to raise revenue within their own borders without taxing enterprise or work.

There is appetite in Scotland for reform of the land tenure system, which still has feudal features. There is already a complete register of land ownership. Land ownership is highly concentrated – 80 per cent of Scotland is owned by 1500 private estates, and 50 per cent of privately owned land is held by just 350 people. As in Estonia, Land Value Taxation is more attractive when foreign nationals own significant amounts of land.

In 2004 the Scottish Green party launched a Bill in the Scottish Parliament to replace Council Tax and Non-Domestic (Business) Rates with Land Value Taxation, though this was defeated. Charges on land values require broad political consensus, and this may be more readily achieved in Scotland than in England as consensus is unlikely where elections are decided by 'first past the post' electoral systems. There is support from the Green and Liberal Democrat parties as well as individual Co-operative and Scottish Nationalist Members of the Scottish Parliament.

England

New Labour embraced the principle of collecting for the common good the market rent of a natural resource – the electromagnetic spectrum. It is difficult to underestimate the importance of this signal that there is no intellectual barrier at government level to stewardship of the environment.

At a local level Oxfordshire County Council has piloted Land Value Taxation but has not taken it forward.

Any government is likely to explore ways to recoup some of the increased land value that arises from granting planning permission or from investment in transport infrastructure. The danger is that the approach to taxation that they use will be applied only where development actually takes place and will be a one-off payment not an ongoing stream of rent. This will have the same problems as have been associated with the Development Land Tax or with Section 106 of the Planning and Compensation Act 1991, and at the same time damage the way that people look on all taxes on land.

One possibility opened up by the Mirrlees review (James Mirrlees et al 2011 Chapter 20:16) is that it recognises Land Value

Taxation as neutral and efficient and recommends deploying it to replace the current system of Non-Domestic (Business) Rates.

Political parties

All the UK political parties believe that, in the current climate, taxes on land values are a potential vote-loser. This is why it is so important that the electorate develops an understanding of the range of advantages of stewardship.

Green

The Green party has been a consistent supporter of Land Value Taxation (as a source of local tax revenue), environmental taxes and charges, and a Citizen's Income (although they suggest that this should be financed from Income Tax). Greens are close in spirit to stewardship and could be its most natural supporters.

Liberal Democrat

Land Value Taxation was an important feature of Lloyd George's 1909 'people's budget', and the Liberal party was always sympathetic to the idea. It is not in their manifesto, and they favour a local Income Tax as a source of local revenue, but the Liberal Democrats do support basing Non-Domestic (Business) Rates on the value of land not overall property value and describe Land Value Taxation as their 'long-term direction of travel'.

The Lib Dem's Action for Land Taxation and Economic Reform (ALTER) includes coalition cabinet members Chris Huhne, Vince Cable and Nick Clegg as President and vice-Presidents.

Labour

The Labour party made serious attempts to introduce Land Value Taxation before the Second World War. Philip Snowden's 1931 budget included Land Value Taxation, but it was blocked by the Conservatives before it could be introduced. Herbert Morrison's 1939 bill introduced Site Value Rating for the London County Council, but this was also blocked by the Conservatives.

The Labour Land Campaign manifesto provides a clear exposition of the benefits of Land Value Taxation. The campaign draws its membership from the Labour Party, Trades Unions and the Co-operative Party, which fields joint candidates with the Labour Party in some seats and includes Land Value Taxation in its manifesto. There were 30 supporters of Land Value Taxation on the opposition benches in the autumn of 2010 including two candidates for the leadership of the Labour party, Andy Burnham and Diane Abbott.

Conservative

The Conservative party has not traditionally been a supporter of Land Value Taxation, though the party under David Cameron has become an advocate for action on environmental issues including tradable emissions permits.

Steve Norris, former Conservative Secretary of State for Transport, was supportive of the principle of land value capture to finance transport infrastructure. There is no support in the parliamentary party for Land Value Taxation in either the UK or Scottish parliaments.

The Bow Group, a Conservative think-tank, published a policy paper by Mark Wadsworth (2006:4) that advocated what he described as Land Value Taxation, though this was to be assessed as 1 per cent per annum of the market value of all residential *properties* (land plus improvements) and with a tax-free allowance of £70,000.

Robin Smith was a Conservative councillor who resigned from the party but hopes to re-join when it adopts a different understanding of private and common property in a free market. He would be worth contacting if you are of a Conservative persuasion.

We have to hope that Conservatives wanting to promote a business-friendly environment, particularly the removal of conventional taxes, will recognise the possibilities offered by stewardship – particularly the substitution of Non-Domestic (Business) Rates by Land Value Taxation.

Scottish Nationalist

The Scottish Nationalists favour raising local revenue by means of a local Income Tax and have opposed Land Value Taxation in Scotland.

The need for political consensus

Landowners have been able to see off a range of land taxes by voting out the government that introduced them.

It is unlikely that any single political party in the UK would take the risk of embarking on the transition to stewardship, or any form of Land Value Taxation, on its own. Political action would need agreement among at least two of the major political parties if it were to be securely and predictably established. This in turn requires a high level of public understanding and support, which is why discussing the ideas is so important.

A political timetable

Tony Vickers (2007:81) has outlined the steps that would need to be taken if a government was elected with a mandate to implement Land Value Taxation in England and Wales. Secondary legislation would be needed to complete the registration of land in England and Wales, and even trials of Land Value Taxation would require primary legislation. This would take a year even if the necessary preparation and desk research had been carried out before a General Election, and he very sensibly proposes local trials that could be evaluated after three years. This would allow the introduction, within a single parliament, of a Land Value Tax that would replace all existing property taxes.

In summary: Any transition needs to be carefully modelled so that the numbers of people losing from transition is kept to the minimum.

There is a need for a widespread popular understanding of the basic principles and advantages of stewardship that can underpin a broad political consensus.

The advantages of stewardship are most easy to recognise when house prices are not rising and when conventional taxes have recently been increased. This is the right time in the economic cycle to explore stewardship

Chapter 16 What can we do straight away?

You, the reader, have already done something – you have contributed the time it has taken you to read some of this book. If you find stewardship convincing, or even interesting, I hope that you will find opportunities to pursue this interest.

This chapter identifies:

- o **information and indicators** to make available
- o areas that need further **research and modelling**
- o **opportunities to raise interest**
- o the requirements for a **pilot site**
- o existing **education and campaign groups** and **political parties**
- o **games** we can play
- o further **reading**.

Information and indicators

We need regular systematic collection and dissemination of information about land. This includes data about property values at the level of individual sites and aggregate measures of the total market rent:

Making Land Registry information available

The development of national gazetteers and the improved access to information held by the Land Registry is very much to be welcomed. It is important that this database be freely available and fully searchable so that we can better understand the value of land in the current ownership economy.

The Land Registry should be tasked with completing the registration of land in England and Wales, separating the value of each property into land and improvement values and indexing these values annually.

Estimating the total market rent of the UK

There is no reliable estimate available for the current total market rent of the land in the UK, and therefore no reliable way to estimate the impact of introducing stewardship or the Universal Income that would be available if the UK was a stewardship economy. The 'total market rent' should be seen as an important macroeconomic variable, and changes over time constitute an important economic indicator. The government needs to estimate this on a regular basis, ideally as satellite accounts in the national accounts (Blue Book) as it does with environmental accounts.

Research and modelling

In order to be able to weigh up the costs and benefits of stewardship we need to carry out feasibility studies of aspects of stewardship – particularly the valuation of improvements independently from land; evidence about the deadweight loss of conventional taxes; modelling of the impact of land values on the economy as a whole; and simulation of the impact of transition on the distribution of income.

Feasibility study of the valuation of improvements

The method proposed in *Stewardship Economy: Private property without private ownership* for assessing the market rent of improved land is absolutely dependent on being able to assess the value of the buildings and improvements. Although surveyors have established methods for doing this, we need to carry out a feasibility study in which surveyors independently assess a wide range of types of properties and ownership interests. This would identify any special types of property for which there are potential difficulties, clarify the amount of work involved in each valuation and establish the precision and accuracy with which valuations can be carried out.

Estimating the deadweight loss of existing taxes

The Treasury uses an estimate of 30 per cent for the deadweight loss of existing taxes, but this may be an underestimate. Fred Harrison (2006a: 208) has established that the Treasury does not have any documentation on how the deadweight loss is calculated and that it does not consider that it would be their role to carry this out. This means that estimating the deadweight loss of UK taxes is an important research task, which should be commissioned by the Treasury so that they are in a position to take note of the results.

Modelling the impact of land values on the economy

Current models of the economy take some account of the market value of land, largely through the impact of house prices on consumer confidence and spending. If the implications of stewardship are to be understood, it will be important to develop models of the economy that include the market rent of land and the possibility of collecting some proportion of this as stewardship fees. This is not just a matter of introducing a new parameter into aggregate models, but of constructing a realistic agent-based dynamic model that would allow exploration of a range of possible reactions of property owners to the introduction of stewardship.

Modelling transition and its impact on the distribution of income

Introducing a Universal Income where there is no existing benefit system is, in principle, simple. Income is distributed to everybody, and it provides a small independent income to provide the basis for life, work and study. Any amount would be helpful, and it could be phased in slowly as funding became available.

Where there is an existing benefit system, introducing a Universal Income involves unravelling parts of a complex existing system of benefits. It is essential to be sure that the new Universal Income does not disadvantage those who are already receiving benefits. It is also important that it is not the well-off who benefit most from the reforms. So, it is important to model a variety of trajectories for transition to the Universal Income and to identify the effect that each has on the distribution of income and wealth.

Opportunities to raise interest and awareness

There are few contemporary issues that would not be affected by stewardship. Taxation of land and the environment has risen up the agenda over the last quarter of a century and there are lots of opportunities to raise interest and awareness of stewardship.

There is a risk, though, in advancing the ideas issue by issue. Why would anybody seriously consider challenging the nature of ownership just to achieve self-financing transport infrastructure, or better allocation of airport landing slots or a shift in the burden of local taxation? The challenge is to locate these individual issues within the picture of a whole stewardship economy.

Non-Domestic (Business) Rates

The Institute for Fiscal Studies commissioned *The Mirrlees Review* to identify the characteristics that would make for a good tax system in an open economy in the 21st century. Amongst its recommendations for reform of the British tax system is the proposal to abolish the current distortionary system of business rates, which discriminates between different sorts of business and disincentivises the development of business property – and to replace it with Land Value Taxation (James Mirrlees et al 2011: Chapter 20 Page 16).

The Liberal Democrats have already adopted the policy of basing business rates on site values rather than on rental values (land plus buildings); and the Labour Land Campaign supports this as a practical step.

The advantages to commercial owners who make efficient use of their land is so clear that it could be expected to be broadly supported by the business community. In spite of the inevitable challenges where land is put to both commercial and residential use, this offers a workable reform that would demonstrate the feasibility, fairness and effectiveness of stewardship.

Tax relief on property investment

From the perspective of stewardship there are few government policies more perverse than exempting property investments from taxation. This operates as a sort of negative Land Value Tax and exacerbates all the worst features of ownership economies including economic injustice and the inflation of property bubbles.

Yet the USA continues to allow tax relief on home mortgage payments. The UK equivalent (Mortgage Interest Relief at Source, MIRAS) was withdrawn in 2000, a reform that had been deemed politically impossible for decades but was actually carried out with very little sustained opposition.

In the UK the mortgage interest payments of a private landlord are deemed to be a business expense, providing tax relief (that is to say, a state subsidy) on these mortgages, one of the major reasons behind the bubble in buy-to-let investments. And in recent years there have been several attempts further to exempt property investments from tax in the UK. In 2006 it was only as a result of public opposition that the government agreed not to allow people to put their holiday homes and buy-to-let properties into self-invested personal pensions (SIPPs) to exempt them from tax. In 2007 listed property companies in the UK became able to turn themselves into Real Estate Investment Trusts and avoid paying taxes. This does reduce some of the perverse incentives in the previous arrangements – for example companies discouraged from actively managing their portfolios because they had to pay Capital Gains Taxes whenever they sold. But increased profits translate into increased land prices not into more affordable properties. The insights in this book should encourage you to oppose tax breaks for investment in land.

Carbon trading

The insights from stewardship provide a clear way to handle the allocation of permits like the European Emissions Trading Scheme

– to make a gradual transition from grandfathering to auctions, and to distribute the revenue on an equal per capita basis as an Environmental Dividend. There are real opportunities for people with an understanding of stewardship to contribute to the debate about carbon pricing, and to use this debate to open up a wider awareness of stewardship.

Rising fuel prices

People are likely to become increasingly angry about rising fuel prices as demand outstrips supply. Those living in rural areas will find that increased transport costs reduce the value of their homes and will recognise that a stewardship economy provides automatic compensation for their increased transport costs in the form of lower stewardship fees.

Where commercial users face unfair competition, for example from European hauliers filling up with cheaper diesel at home for their British deliveries, there may need to be legislative support – for example to require all vehicles to fill up on leaving the UK. People will recognise the value of the Environmental Dividend in offsetting prices that will rise as commercial users of fuel, including road hauliers and farmers, pass the cost of their fuel on to the consumer.

If rising fuel prices are to trigger support for stewardship it will be important to emphasise that a stewardship economy would need to provide subsidies for home insulation.

Negative equity

Falling house prices initially make it difficult to discuss measures that hold house prices down. But as people start to ask, 'how can we stop this from happening again?', there can be a serious debate not just about reckless bank lending but about the quasi-cyclical pattern of house prices and the way in which stewardship removes the risk of negative equity.

Transport infrastructure

In the wake of the bailout of the banking system and the subsequent recession, spending on transport infrastructure is being cut. Self-funding infrastructure provides both a mechanism for increased funding for transport and an introduction to the wider benefits of stewardship.

New housing developments

There will continue to be discussion of how to replace Section 106 and the Community Infrastructure Levy with a more satisfactory way to enable local authorities to capture some of the planning gain from developments to fund infrastructure provision. This will provide the opportunity to discuss funding mechanisms that are ongoing rather than one-off, and that tap into the land value created by local authority investments outside these new developments.

Affordable housing

The challenge of providing affordable housing will remain and become more of an issue when house prices rise. Discussions of affordable housing always offer the opportunity to separate out the issues of owning a house from that of owning the land on which it stands; and so to the benefits of Community Land Trusts, land as something other than a commodity, and stewardship.

Retirement communities

Community Land Trusts separate the ownership of land from the ownership of buildings and could provide a way to introduce a voluntary form of stewardship. They require a benefactor to donate the land at the outset and an affluent group of pensioners could choose to self-fund their retirement housing as a Community Land Trust, perhaps using the reduction in their Inheritance Tax liabilities to donate land for affordable housing.

A pilot site?

A pilot could be carried out at the level of local government, with Council Tax and Non-Domestic (Business) Rates being replaced by stewardship fees.

If a pilot is to include one of the main features of stewardship, the reduction or removal of other forms of taxation, it has to be sponsored by a national government. A whole country might decide to adopt stewardship if there was a need for land reform. It might be attractive to a country that wants to set itself up as a tax haven. Or it might be attractive to a new state that had a mandate to establish a fair economic order. Could it happen in Scotland as Holyrood takes on greater autonomy in managing the economy in Scotland?

The most likely site for a pilot is a local area in which a government wants to see economic development. It should only be carried out in an area that is able to demonstrate high levels of local support. It would need to be somewhere to which it is practical for businesses to locate, and which includes access to international transport connections. It would need a variety of housing, including housing attractive to the rich who would want to live there to avoid taxation.

China provides an interesting example of an economy that has tolerated and encouraged very different economic regimes in different areas, most obviously Hong Kong. It has demonstrated that it is capable of making bold changes in the social and economic spheres – might it be capable of piloting stewardship?

Education and campaign groups

Land Value Taxation

The International Union (www.theIU.org) is the main international organisation devoted to promoting the thinking of Henry George. It is a non-governmental organisation with special consultative status at the United Nations 'Economic and Social Council.

The Henry George Foundation (www.henrygeorgefoundation.org) is the main UK organisation providing research, education and advocacy for Land Value Taxation. Its purpose is to spread understanding of the writings of Henry George. It organises classes and conferences, publishes the magazine *Land and Liberty*, and the Links page on its website connects with other organisations sympathetic to Georgist thinking. It has a 'library group' that meets at the School of Economic Science on Friday afternoons.

The School of Economic Science (www.schooleconomicscience.org) provides courses on Economics that include discussion of Land Value Taxation.

Lincoln Institute of Land Policy (www.lincolninst.edu) is based in Cambridge, Massachusetts. It is a leading international research institution seeking to improve the quality of public debate about the use, regulation and taxation of land. It distributes a free newsletter covering a wide range of land use and land policy issues.

The Robert Schalkenbach Foundation (www.schalkenbach.org) publishes books and articles about Land Value Taxation, including a modernised version of Henry George's *Progress and Poverty*.

James Robertson (www.jamesrobertson.com) has been at the heart of the development of thinking about the New Economy for over 30 years and was one of the founders of the New Economics Foundation. He has written many books that advocate, as part of their proposals, Land Value Taxation and a Citizens 'Income; and has been at the forefront of thinking about monetary reform and alternatives to debt-based money. The Links page on his website puts you in touch with a very wide range of initiatives and groups, and he has a regular email newsletter.

Fred Harrison (https://shepheardwalwyn.com/fred-harrison-author/) the author of many books on Land Value Taxation and deputy president of the International Union, provides video downloads, podcasts and a blog on contemporary economic issues.

The Systemic Fiscal Reform Group was a Cambridge-based think-tank inspired by James Robertson. Adrian Wrigley (died 2013) developed the intriguing suggestion that a form of Land Value

Taxation could be introduced on a voluntary plot-by-plot basis. The owner of the plot would place a Location Value Covenant on the land that creates an obligation on its owners in perpetuity to pay an annual fee, indexed to land values, to a public body in exchange for removal of property-linked taxes and perhaps benefits.

Alanna Hartzok of the Earth Rights Institute and the International Union developed an online course on Land Value Capture that has enrolled over 500 students from 80 countries.

Andy Wightman (www.andywightman.com) is a writer and researcher specialising in land reform, land tenure and land ownership; and is a leading advocate of land reform in Scotland. He maintains an active blog, which is particularly strong on Scottish issues.

The Land Value Taxation Campaign (www.landvaluetax.org) is a single-issue organisation based in the UK. Its expertise is in implementing Land Value Taxation, and its website provides a commentary on current affairs from the perspective of Land Value Taxation.

Land is Free (www.landisfree.co.uk) provides topic papers on a range of issues related to Land Value Taxation.

Universal Income

The Citizen's Income Trust (www.citizensincome.org) promotes discussion of the feasibility of a citizen's income in the UK through its newsletter and seminars.

The Global Basic Income Foundation (www.globalincome.org) promotes the policy of distributing a Universal Income to all people in all countries, starting at a level of $10 per month per person.

Climate change

The New Economics Foundation (www.neweconomics.org) is a think-and-do tank that combines promotion of local economic and social sustainability with campaigns and publications on issues such as Community Land Trusts and Climate Change.

The Foundation for the Economics of Sustainability (FEASTA) (www.feasta.org) is based in Dublin and promotes the change to a truly sustainable society. It has working groups and online discussion groups focusing on a wide range of sustainability issues, including climate change and the land.

Inequalities

The Equality Trust (www.equalitytrust.org.uk) educates about the consequences of inequalities and campaigns for a more equal society.

Further reading

To pursue these ideas in more detail you may want to take a look at the other books in the series and Shepheard-Walwyn, who publish many of the UK books on Land Value Taxation, have a useful website (www.ethicaleconomics.org.uk).

The authors that I find myself recommending to people interested in stewardship include:

Peter Barnes. *Who owns the sky?* (2001) is one of the most compelling introductions to the concept of stewardship, although not using the word, focusing on property rights applied to the atmosphere. It is reasoned, passionate and readable.

Henry George. The hugely influential *Progress and poverty* (1879) is a fascinating introduction to the rationale for Land Value Taxation.

Fred Harrison has written extensively about Land Value Taxation for a British audience for the last three decades. I particularly like his book on transport and its funding, *Wheels of fortune* (2006a).

Thomas Paine. *Agrarian Justice* (1797a) is only a short tract, but he puts all the passion and reason that you would expect from him into this proposal for a form of what I would call stewardship.

James Robertson. *Benefits and taxes* (1994) sets out a timetable for a tax shift to Land Value Taxation and a benefit shift to

Citizens 'Income; and (with Joseph Huber) *Creating new money* (2000) presents a proposal for monetary reform.

John Stewart. *Prime Minister* (2010) is the third of his political novels and the most compelling. A young prime minister and coalition government face economic meltdown, against the background of traditional social mores. The challenges, discussions and interviews provide a clear and accessible introduction to Land Value Taxation. It makes a good holiday read and a handy gift – you may be able to interest others in the ideas by slipping them a copy.

Tony Vickers. *Location matters: recycling Britain's wealth* (2007) provides a concise introduction to Land Value Taxation from a contemporary British political perspective.

Games

One way to help people to get a feel for stewardship and its advantages over ownership is to play well-designed games.

The popular board game Monopoly®, brought to the mass market by Parker Brothers in 1933, involves buying and selling properties, developing them and collecting rents. The board layout and underlying concept is taken from The Landlord's Game which was patented in 1904 by an American Quaker, Elizabeth Magie, who designed it with the specific intention of teaching the players about Land Value Taxation.

https://en.wikipedia.org/wiki/The_Landlord%27s_Game

Another alternative is to conduct a thought experiment. Imagine playing a conventional game of Monopoly®. When all the sites are owned, introduce a new player who owns no land and experiences the position of the landless and of young people in an ownership economy. Do they stand any chance of surviving?

The Landlord's Game was designed to be played twice – first using 'landlords' rules', then using 'prosperity rules'. Why not get out your Monopoly® board and play it twice, using two sets of house rules – ownership and stewardship – and compare the two experiences.

The ownership rules are a modification of the official rules so that the game is closer to the reality of an ownership economy. There is no requirement that a player owns all the sites of the same colour before they can improve it. Only one house can be put on each site – as Robin Smith has pointed out, the standard rules allocate a far greater proportion of the revenue from a developed property to the buildings than is realistic. And all properties are owned at the start.

Under the stewardship rules each time the player passes GO they pay the stewardship fees on all their land and collect their Universal Income. A possible set of rules are set out opposite.

House rules for Monopoly® - ownership and stewardship

Play in the usual way, with the following modifications:

Ownership rules

Deal out the site cards face-up among the players, so all properties are owned. Give each player half the money set out in the official rules. Players receive NO income on passing GO.

Each move

All actions take place during a player's turn, which begins by throwing the dice and moving their counter. Pay the standard Monopoly amount to the owner (if any) of the site on which you land. Think of payments for undeveloped sites as rent, and payments for developed sites as a combination of rent for land and rental for the buildings. The player may also carry out none or more of the following:

- ❏ Develop ANY of the sites they own with a maximum of one house, purchased from the bank. The player does not have to have landed on that site. There is no requirement to own all the sites of that colour.
- ❏ Buy any site that the bank holds, at face value. Sell any property (site and/or house) to the bank at face value.

Stewardship rules

The stewardship rules are the same as the ownership rules but prescribes new behaviour on passing GO, when the player:

- ❏ Pays the rent (undeveloped) on ALL their own properties to the Land Stewardship Trust (GO square).
- ❏ Collects an equal share of the money held by the Land Stewardship Trust (for example take ¼ of the money if there are 4 players).

Do you find that the game using the stewardship rules leads to undeveloped sites being released by their owners? Are the stewardship rules less likely than the ownership rules to bankrupt the losers and produce an overall winner? Does the game become endless and perhaps tedious? Would you like the real economy to behave that way too?

Another instructive game is the online virtual reality 'Second Life' in which individuals and corporations can acquire a presence. Virtual land is bought for US dollars from the owners of the website but can then be bought and sold for the local virtual currency, Linden dollars, which has an exchange rate with US dollars. In games of this sort, different plots acquire different values, and land speculation has been one of the main economic activities that has developed. A virtual reality of this sort would be a fascinating environment into which to introduce a transition to stewardship; both to understand how people might respond and to familiarise them with the principles.

In summary: This chapter has identified some of the steps we could take in an ownership economy to explore and prepare for stewardship.

If you would like to pursue the ideas in more detail you may want to look at the other books, available through http://stewardship-economy.org/stewardship-economy/

Whatever you decide to do at this stage, I hope that your view of the world has been disturbed and that you can see new possibilities. You have already made a contribution by taking the time to read at least some of this book, and I hope that you will want to talk to other people about what you have read. If every reader talks to two other people and passes their copy on to somebody else...........

FURTHER INFORMATION

Frequently Answered Questions

Are stewardship fees fair?

Who gets the land?

What's to stop the rich from monopolising the best land?

The rich will be in a position to monopolise the best land in a stewardship economy, just as they are in an ownership economy. The difference is that they will pay for the privilege and everybody else benefits. That certainly seems fairer than the situation in an ownership economy where the landowners monopolise not only the use of the land, but its market rent and any increase in its market value.

Farmers

As 85 per cent of the UK is used for agriculture or forestry, wouldn't stewardship be unfair to farmers?

The fee that a steward pays depends on the market rent of the land, not on the number of acres. Each acre of land in a city is worth hundreds or even thousands of times more than an acre of farmland. Agricultural and forestry land make up just 5 per cent of the value of all land in the UK, and so only 5 per cent of the revenue from stewardship fees would come from agriculture and forestry. But the economics of farming would change significantly.

Landowners

Surely it is unfair to impose heavier taxes on landowners than on others?

In a mature stewardship economy, fees equal to 100 per cent of the market rent of the land would be entirely fair. 'Landowners' would not be disadvantaged in such an economy because there would be none.

During transition from an ownership economy, it would be unfair to penalise landowners, which is why the stewardship fees apply only to the increase in the market rent of land that occurs after the beginning of the transition.

A widow living in a large house

Is it fair that the stewardship fees people pay do not depend on their ability to pay them?

The situation that immediately occurs to readers when they encounter proposals for a charge on land values is that of a widow on a fixed income living in the old family house that is now too big for her needs in an expensive part of town, who finds that, through no fault of her own, she can't afford the stewardship fee. Perhaps land values have risen dramatically through gentrification, or because the area is sought by developers.

There is a genuine sense of unfairness in this situation. The widow no longer has enough income to pay the stewardship fee. In one sense, she does have the 'ability to pay' as she is the steward of an asset (the land) that she could rent out for the same amount as the stewardship fee she has to pay. But, of course, this potential income is not available to her while she continues to live there.

The widow lives alone, so there is only one Universal Income coming into the household. She personifies change and deteriorating fortune, and in a world of 'rational' economic agents the appropriate response would be for her to move to live on a less valuable site. But the widow also personifies vulnerability and attachment. Having lived in this house for many years, the house is familiar and full of memories. It is located in a neighbourhood and a web of social relationships, and to move would rob her of all this. We all recognise that the attachment we make to a house and garden is uniquely strong in our relationships with the inanimate world. For this reason, stewardship is not acceptable without some sort of qualification that would make it as easy as possible for the widow to remain in her home.

At the very least, the tax system must allow her to use the value of the building (her positive equity) to defer payment of the stewardship fee. The Land Stewardship Trust could simply roll over the payment until it is paid when she leaves. Or she might sell the building to a third party who will maintain it and rent it back to her as long as she wants to stay; and use the capital to purchase an annuity to pay the rent and stewardship fee, in the same way that people now do to purchase residential care. In either way the widow herself does not suffer, though her family inherit less.

During transition it would be necessary to provide protection for people whose equity in the house is insufficient to provide for the payments of stewardship fees, for example by making housing benefit available to stewards.

We inevitably view this dilemma from the perspective of an ownership economy. Ownership economies have encouraged us to become financially attached to our homes. In the long run, the trend in land prices is upwards and home ownership in the UK is seen as an investment and a gift to be passed on to the next generation, rather than as a form of consumption. For the owner-occupier, the home has often been the main source of financial, as well as physical, security – though it can be a false sense of security when homes fall in value, develop negative equity and are repossessed by mortgage lenders.

Living in a stewardship economy would alter our sense of priorities. Here the source of genuine security is the right to an equal share of the stewardship fees of all land, in the form of a Universal Income. People growing up in a stewardship economy may be less strongly attached to a particular site than we are today. When we think of the widow, we imagine that she has bought her house in an ownership economy with current expectations and suddenly finds herself subjected to a stewardship fee.

In an established stewardship economy, especially once it had been in operation for a few generations, people anticipate the need to move home or to set funds aside during working life. One purpose, after all, of stewardship is to ensure that land is put to the best possible use, and all sorts of households in the UK live in homes with many more bedrooms than they need. Over the course of time housing providers would supply housing units with a mix of sizes, allowing people to move to a suitably sized home without disrupting their social networks.

A millionaire

What about a millionaire who pays little or no tax?

Even in a stewardship economy most wealthy people are likely to occupy the prime sites, both for their homes and for their businesses. People who have wealth in an ownership economy generally spend a significant amount of it on the place where they live. In part this is because home ownership is a good investment in an ownership economy. But it is largely because we spend to improve our quality of life – and a pleasant and convenient place to live is high on most people's list of priorities.

Current inequalities in both wealth and land ownership are greater than inequalities in income. As Adam Smith anticipated, a tax on land values 'would in general fall heaviest upon the rich' (1776 Volume III Book V Chapter II: 236). But it will not do so in absolutely every case.

Exemptions

What land should be exempted from the need to pay a stewardship fee? Would charities, churches and other faith buildings, local and national government all be exempt?

It is very important that no land at all is exempted from stewardship. Local and national government need every possible incentive to make good use of their land. Excluding particular sorts of owner, like charities and faith groups, would lead to these becoming the new tax havens. Institutions like these, whose state subsidy in ownership economies is provided through tax exemptions, need a direct subsidy in a stewardship economy (Chapter 8).

Why do you have to tax 100 per cent of the market rent?

Stewardship allocates land to whoever is prepared to offer the greatest compensation to others for excluding them from it. This means that the steward actually has to pay the whole amount as compensation. This allocation mechanism also works for the proposed transition approach, but it would not work if the steward had to bid, say, half the market rent.

Surely it's not fair to tax savings or wealth

In a stewardship economy land is not a form of private wealth or savings. Indeed, there are ideally no taxes at all on savings or investment as there are in ownership economies.

Does it redistribute wealth effectively?

Surely the aim of a tax-benefit system is to redistribute wealth from the rich to the poor?

The rationale underlying stewardship is not the redistribution of wealth, though that is the likely outcome. The intention is to provide everybody with an equal share of the wealth of the natural world. Any re-distributive effect arises because the rich use more than their share of the natural world.

Why not tax all forms of economic rent?

One reason for taxing land and the natural world is that its supply is fixed (inelastic). Vilfredo Pareto pointed out that land is not alone in having an inelastic supply and developed the idea that any factor of production whose supply is inelastic will receive what he called an 'economic rent'. This is 'the surplus received by any factor of production above the amount needed to keep that factor in its present production.' Thus, if certain skills are inherently rare, people with these skills earn an economic rent. Or if a certain wine or painting has unique qualities, much of its price can be attributed to economic rent.

The ethical reason for not taxing other forms of economic rent is that land and the natural world are assets on which we all have an equal claim, and which should be shared by everybody; while footballers skills are their own and the ownership of a painting by Leonardo da Vinci can be traced back to its creator through a series of transactions.

One pragmatic reason for not taxing other forms of economic rent is that the supply of highly skilled workers may not be as inelastic as you imagine – taxing their income may reduce the amount of work they do or drive them into tax exile.

The proposal to tax all forms of economic rent is usually made not by people who genuinely advocate doing so, but by those who are using the argument as a *reductio ad absurdam* to attack taxation of land.

Isn't this just communism?

If the state collects the market rent of land then the state really owns the land – this is communism.

Stewardship certainly doesn't look like capitalism as we know it, but it isn't communism either. Stewardship can support socialism just as it can support libertarianism, but not the collective ownership of property that characterises communism. Land is held in trust in a stewardship economy, but each plot is private property, because each steward can make use of the land as they wish without reference to the will of the collective (apart from the usual planning regulations).

Stewardship is closely related to Henry George's Single Tax, and Karl Marx could see that this is not communism – he

perceptively described Henry George as 'the capitalists' last ditch '
(Henry Hyndman 1911:281).

Would it work?

What happens if the valuation is wrong?

*If the stewardship fee is set at the wrong level, surely the land will
not be used efficiently? If it is set too high, the land will lie idle; if
it is set too low, the owner will get an unwarranted subsidy
compared with competitors and will lack the incentive to use it to
the full. Errors in valuation distort land use.*

This is a serious question that advocates of Land Value Taxation
have sometimes failed to take sufficiently seriously. It applies
particularly to proposals that would set the stewardship fee for a
plot of land on the basis of the opinion of a state-appointed valuer.

If the fee were to be set higher than the market rent then it would
not be profitable to use the site. Setting stewardship fees too high
would damage the economy, and this could be a real danger during
the downswing of an economic cycle when market rents are falling.
If the fee is set too low, the revenue from stewardship fees would
be reduced; and there is also a risk that purchasers would offer
illegal payments to secure stewardship of the site.

It is important that the stewardship fee is determined, wherever
possible, by the market not by a valuer; and that it is flexible, able
to fall or rise depending on the state of the general economy or on
local factors.

The annual re-valuation using comparables that have been exposed
to the market can never be perfect – but neither is an ownership
economy, which has its own ways of distorting land use. And the
steward can always appeal to valuation by the market.

Is it possible to value blocks of offices and flats?

The task for a valuer in the new land market is to estimate the
Depreciated Replacement Cost of the entire building and then to

apportion this amongst the various interests in the building. The market rent of each interest is then established independently in the market, and the market rent of the whole site is the sum of the market rents of each of these interests. This is described in more detail elsewhere. As freeholds and head leases become more of a liability than an asset they tend to be passed on to the occupying lease-holders, and the ownership structure of the property becomes more streamlined.

Wouldn't it destroy the land market?

If 100 per cent of the market rent is collected as stewardship fees, the market value of land falls to zero. How is stewardship transferred from one person to another? Surely the land market will be destroyed?

Land Value Taxes have been successfully assessed and collected in ownership economies at up to 25 per cent of market rent, calculated as a proportion of either the market value of the land or its market rent.

Different arrangements are needed when 100 per cent of the market rent is collected, as the market value of land in a stewardship economy is indeed zero.

The land market as we know it, in the form of direct purchases by a buyer from a seller, does not exist in a stewardship economy. It is replaced by a new land market, in which the Land Stewardship Trust transfers properties at auction. This is more open, transparent and efficient than property markets in ownership economies.

Won't it erode the tax base?

If the market value of land is zero, what is there to tax? The stewardship fee is determined in a new land market). It depends on the gross market rent, not the market value, of land.

Won't landowners go on strike?

The experience of taxes on the increase in land value that occurs when planning permission is granted for development, like the notorious Development Land Tax, led to landowners boycotting development and waiting for the government to fall and the tax to be removed. Although stewardship is clearly different, isn't the proposed transition, with stewardship fees equal to the increase in market rent, going to run into the same problems?

There are two big differences between the transition mechanism and Development Land Tax. One is that it applies to all land, not just to land under development. The other is that the market rent is collected on an ongoing monthly basis, not as a single payment at the time of disposal or development. There is nothing to gain from delay.

Is rent really a surplus?

Adam Smith (1776 Volume I Book I Chapter XI: 217) pointed out that, while high wages and profits cause the price of commodities to be high, it is the high price of commodities that causes high rents. David Ricardo was clear that 'corn is not high because a rent is paid but a rent is paid because corn is high.' (1817: Chapter II: 62) – and this is accepted by orthodox economists (Paul Samuelson & William Nordhaus 1992:265). The idea that rent is a surplus can, however, feel counterintuitive.

The reason is that, from the perspective of those of us who pay it, rent is not a 'surplus' but a fixed and unavoidable cost like any other. The trader in the city centre has to pay the rent up front, and then struggle to make a profit or move to a cheaper site. In a similar way the rent or purchase price of a house is, from the householders' point of view, a 'given' that determines where they can live.

But what is true when seen from the perspective of an individual is not necessarily true when seen from the perspective of the whole – to argue that way is the fallacy of composition. Looking at the economy as a whole it is clear that rent is a price that depends on the supply and demand for land – and demand will depend on the profit that the site could be expected to generate or the enjoyment that the owner gets from it. If traders find rents are higher than their profits they will move away, and rents will fall with the level of demand.

Is the supply of land really fixed (price-inelastic)?

If the price of a manufactured good rises, producers will supply more. Much of the reason for the price-inelasticity of land is that 'they ain't making it no more' (attributed to Mark Twain).

Of course, it is possible to point to examples where land is being created or discovered – *terra firma* comes and goes at its boundaries with the sea, and new aspects of the natural world (radio spectrum and satellite orbits for example) are recognised as science and technology advances. But these are of small importance when compared with the amount of land that is always there.

And the price-inelasticity of land does not depend solely on it being more-or-less fixed in amount. Inelasticity means that the amount supplied on the market does not increase or decrease as its price rises or falls.

The amount of land available on the market does change. Sometimes there are few houses on the market; sometimes there is a glut. But the amount of land offered on the market is related to a complex set of factors including the rate of increase, or decrease, in prices – not to the price itself.

For the many people and organisations that own land because they need it for living or production, high land prices are no incentive to sell, as they would need to buy somewhere else instead. And for those who have invested in land, a higher price is usually a signal to hold on to their investment, not to sell it – except at the top of the cycle when there are fears that prices may fall. The supply of land on the market is determined by confidence and expectations and does not vary directly with price – it is price-inelastic.

How would it affect me?

How transition would affect individuals depends critically on the path that is chosen. Its implications for a wide range of families, and the distributional impact on the whole population, would need to be extensively modelled so that the chosen path is one that does no harm to the poorest.

But to get a sense of what an established stewardship economy might be like, let us indulge in a thought experiment. Suppose stewardship is introduced overnight into the UK, leaving the current tax-benefit system in place and government spending unchanged:

How much would my stewardship fee be?

As a very rough approximation take the value of the home that you own; divide this by 20 to give an approximate annual market rent of the whole property and divide this by three to give you an approximate annual market rent of the land. So, if you own a home currently valued at £180,000, your annual stewardship fee would be, very approximately, £3000 – less in areas of low land value where land makes up a smaller proportion of the value, and more in areas of high land value. It would be zero if you were renting.

How much would the Universal Income be?

Taking land values at 2007 levels, stewardship fees would total around £180 billion per year. Distributed on an equal per capita basis this would provide about £56 per week (approximately £2900 per person per year); or alternatively it could provide £50 per week for children, £40 per week for adults of working age and £100 per week for the over-65s. That would be in addition to existing benefits. As mentioned above, this assumes existing taxes and benefits are retained. This figure will rise substantially as taxes are reduced (resulting in increased economic activity) and existing benefits replaced (see book 7).

Are there unexpected consequences?

Would it cause over-development?

Stewardship brings underused land into better – that is to say, greater – use. Will it force the over-use and over-development of sites that would be better left relatively under-developed –

businesses of low economic but high social value, low-rent housing and workspace?

Stewardship applies a financial pressure to put each site to the best possible use. Across the country as a whole, however, this brings into use derelict land, underused land and second homes. The new availability of this land relieves some of the pressure on sites of low economic but high social value.

If the pressure to develop these sites nevertheless proves to be excessive, it may be necessary to use the planning system to restrict the use to which those plots of land are put.

Would a Universal Income discourage work?

We know for sure that the system of unemployment benefits with which we are familiar in the UK discourages people on benefit from working. Mass unemployment, combined with a conditional benefit system that actually requires people *not* to work at all if they want to receive unemployment benefit, provides perhaps the worst of all possible solutions. For some people up to 95 per cent of earned income is taken away from them through taxation and withdrawal of benefit when they enter work, and even the most ambitious reforms of the coalition government are to reduce this to 60 per cent. The benefit system actually makes it illogical for many people to work.

I believe that we should design the benefit system so that it allows those who want to work to do so without impediment.

Most individuals with a small independent income from the Universal Income would want or need to earn more, and they could do so with no more than 30 to 40 per cent of it being withdrawn during transition. Some of these people might work fewer hours per week than they would in an ownership economy, but most would probably work just as much, or even more when Income Tax is lifted.

There is also a big difference between choosing not to work and being excluded from work. Unemployment in an ownership economy results in a contraction of choices and possibilities, while being without paid work in a stewardship economy might be a positive choice and an expansion of possibilities.

Would people squander their Universal Income?

A stewardship economy provides people with opportunities for self-determination not protection from themselves. There certainly have been examples where the provision of unearned income has had a destabilising effect, particularly if it is introduced rapidly or as a one-off payment. A win on the lottery or a sudden influx of oil money to a country may be spent on displays of wealth, for example. But this is largely a problem of rapid transition.

Perhaps it would be best to ask parents whether they squander their Child Benefit and pensioners whether they squander the Basic State Pension. About a third of the recipients of the Alaska Dividend Distribution Scheme spend it all, about half the recipients save it all and the rest spend some and save some (Peter Barnes 2001:71). In Namibia, after introduction of the Basic Income, hunger and undernutrition fell and the use of (fee-paying) schools and health clinics rose. Economic activity and household income increased as people were able to purchase the means of making an income (Basic Income Grant Coalition 2009:3).

Would stewardship fees be passed on to tenants and consumers?

Taxes on things like sales or wages, for example, are passed on to the consumer - remember what happens to pump prices when tax on petrol is increased at the budget. Won't the landlord just pass the cost of the stewardship fee on to the tenant, and the tenant then pass it on to customers through higher prices?

Taxes on sales and wages are passed on to consumers because they fall equally on all competitors, competing products or workers. Charges on the market rent of land cannot be passed on because they fall very unequally.

At the marginal site (the least productive site at which anybody would choose to engage in production) there will be no rent, and thus no fee or charge, to pay. A high-value site commands a higher rent than a marginal site because it can charge more for goods or sell more of them. At these sites, however, any attempt by the landlord to pass the fee on to the tenant by asking more than the market rent will fail, as no tenant is going to be able to make enough profit to pay it. It is competition from sites with lower market rents that makes it impossible to pass stewardship fees on to the consumer.

Adam Smith distinguished between the two components of the rent of a house, building rent ('rental 'in our terms) and ground rent ('market rent') (Adam Smith 1776 Volume III Book V Chapter II: 232). Since his time there has been general agreement amongst orthodox economists that taxes and charges on the market rent cannot be passed on:

'Ground rents are a still more proper subject of taxation than the rents of houses. A tax upon ground-rents would not raise the rents of houses. It would fall altogether on the owner of the ground rent, who acts always as a monopolist, and exacts the greatest rent that can be got for the use of his ground ....Whether the tax was to be advanced by the inhabitant, or by the owner of the ground, would be of little importance. The more the inhabitant was obliged to pay for the tax, the less he would incline to pay for the ground; so that the final payment of the tax would fall altogether on the owner of the ground-rent' (Adam Smith 1776 Volume III Book V Chapter II:238).

'A land-tax, levied in proportion to the rent of land, and varying with every variation of rent, is in effect a tax on rent; and as such a tax will not apply to that land which yields no rent, nor to the produce of that capital which is employed on that land with a view to profit merely, and which never pays rent, it will not in any way affect the price of raw produce, but will fall wholly on the landlords' (David Ricardo 1817:232).

Would stewardship fees reduce profitability?

You often see business premises, such as shops in a city, unoccupied because of the heavy burden of rent and rates. Surely a stewardship fee would reduce the profitability of enterprises just as the rent and rates do?

If the stewardship fee for a site was incorrectly set at a level above the market rent it would indeed lead to that site being unoccupied. That is why it is so important to design the practicalities of valuation so that the stewardship fee really does equal the market rent using direct market mechanisms wherever possible.

A landlord who rents out their land to another enterprise would, if transported from an ownership to a stewardship economy, suffer from having to pay a stewardship fee equal to the market rent.

Their income from the land element of their property, net of stewardship fees, would be zero.

A business that rents its land from a landlord would be unaffected by any liability to pay the stewardship fee, which is paid by the landlord and not passed on to the tenant. If Government revenue from stewardship fees is used to fund reductions in taxes such as Income Tax, National Insurance contributions, VAT and Corporation Tax then a stewardship economy would *increase* the profitability of such a firm.

A business that owns its own land would pay no more in stewardship fees than a competitor who is a tenant pays in rent, or a competitor who is buying their site with a loan pays in interest on the loan.

So, the only businesses whose profitability is compromised by the introduction of stewardship fees are those who had previously been receiving a hidden subsidy as the outright owner of their site.

Would people take to the road?

Wouldn't people take to the road to avoid paying the stewardship fee, increasing the number of travellers?

Most people at present pay rent or a mortgage, and this doesn't drive them to travel. The stewardship fee is simply a form of rent that is paid to all of us rather than to a landlord.

If it's such a good idea, why aren't we doing it already?

Hasn't it been tried before and failed?

From the time of the earliest written records, in Mesopotamia, public revenue was raised from lands that were designated to support religious and state institutions. But as palace rule weakened around 2300 BCE the royal and public landholdings passed into private ownership (Michael Hudson 2000:9). People have a powerful temptation and a long history of capturing the rents from land and natural resources for their own private benefit.

The British, unable and unwilling to challenge land ownership at home, understood the advantages of raising state revenue from land rather than from conventional taxes and put this into place in many of their colonies. Land Value Taxation has been applied in Australia, New Zealand, South Africa and the state of Pennsylvania. Other countries that have made successful use of relatively low levels of Land Value Taxes include Denmark and the Baltic States.

In the UK a range of taxes has been applied to land including the Council Tax, Non-Domestic (Business) Rates, Development Land Tax and so on. None of these has taken the form of a tax on the market rent of land and all have had quite predictable adverse economic impacts (Tony Vickers 2007: 69).

Charges amounting to 100 per cent of the market rent of land are untried. However, in Singapore and Hong Kong the state does not use Land Value Taxation, but it does retain the freehold of much of the land and derives a great deal of its revenue from leases, providing the economic basis for their vibrant low-tax economies.

Also, the auction of licences to use the radio spectrum provides an example of the application to the environment of a charge equal to 100 per cent of the market rent.

Doesn't this belong to an agricultural age?

Land may be important in an agricultural society, but surely not in an industrial or knowledge-based economy?

Access to land can certainly be a matter of life and death in agricultural economies. But land values play a central, if often unrecognised, role in the functioning of industrial and knowledge-based economies. The value an acre of land that is occupied by factories, shops, offices or homes dwarfs that of an acre of agricultural land.

'Location, location, location 'are said to be the most important factors identified by estate agents as determining the value of a home; and everyone is aware of the enormous differences in price for the same sort of house in different parts of a country. The same is true for commercial and industrial land. Land value is largely determined by location and the presence or absence of planning restrictions.

Land and natural resources are important in all economies. The practical and ethical issue of who should benefit from them is a key choice, no matter what the level of complexity of the society.

In a globalised world it is difficult to tax capital, business and high earners, as these are all highly mobile. Raising revenue from land and the environment is, even at a very pragmatic level, increasingly essential in the 21st century.

Isn't it wacky?

Don't orthodox economists regard Land Value Taxation as 'wacky', an object of fun rather than a serious proposition?

Land Value Taxation is used in several countries around the world, albeit at no more than 20 per cent of market rent. The UK government is currently interested in using land value gains to finance transport infrastructure projects and the Scottish Executive has debated Land Value Taxation.

Orthodox economists have reasonable and serious criticisms of the impact of Land Value Taxes on the land market and land use, particularly about the erosion of the tax base, destruction of the land market and the reduction of profitability. These criticisms are addressed by the design of the new land market. Stewardship deserves serious consideration, as it provides a unifying theory and practice that can inform a wide range of contemporary issues.

Glossary

See Book 7 for the full glossary

Here I set out the way that I use a number of key terms – land, environment, natural world, rent, market rent, market value, true cost, stewardship, stewardship fee, Universal Income and stewardship economy:

Land, the environment and the natural world

This book emphasises the fundamental distinction between three very different categories – people; artefacts (things made by people); and everything that occurs in nature without the intervention of people. I use the term **'natural world'** to refer to this third category – **all those sites, spaces, forces and opportunities that occur in nature without the intervention of people.**

I divide the 'natural world' into 'land' and 'the environment'. **'Land' is the solid surface of the planet**. It includes agricultural, urban, residential, industrial, and commercial land, public spaces, highways, derelict sites, moorland and wilderness. Land comprises the location, described by its co-ordinates, and the topsoil.

This use of the term 'land 'is close to the everyday common-sense use of the word, but different from its meanings in both law and economics. It is close to the way that it is used in writings on surveying and valuing and is probably what is meant by 'land 'in the International Accounting Standard on Leases (IAS 7) although the term is not explicitly defined there. The Royal Institute of Chartered Surveyors (RICS 2006:7) interprets land as comprising the location combined with the physical ability and legal right to use and construct improvements on the site.

This differs from its usage in economics, including writings on Land Value Taxation, where 'land' is used to mean what I call in this book the 'natural world' and includes the oceans, atmosphere, mineral reserves and so on.

It also differs from the legal meaning of 'land', which includes any changes ('improvements') brought about by people such as buildings, drainage, irrigation systems, roads and bridges. By contrast, I explicitly exclude improvements from 'land' (although improvements may eventually merge with the land, as explained below). Most places you can think of, then, are in this terminology a combination of 'land' and 'improvements'.

'The environment 'refers to all aspects of the natural world that are not land. It includes bodies of water including oceans, seas, lakes and rivers. It includes spaces below the surface, such as the seabed, aquifers, deposits of minerals and hydrocarbons and the spaces occupied by underground railways, cables, drains and so on. It includes spaces above the surface – the electromagnetic spectrum, the atmosphere, the ozone layer, airspace, satellite orbits and indeed the whole of the solar system – but not the space occupied by buildings or improvements attached to the land. 'Land' and the 'environment' refer to a space, to its potential use and to its naturally occurring contents. These may include natural resources (such as topsoil, water, minerals, fossil fuels, wild animals, naturally occurring plants and trees and biodiversity); sinks (space to dump household waste, sewage, industrial and agricultural pollutants, carbon dioxide, radioactive isotopes etc.); and amenities (aspects of the natural world that are consumed directly rather than being transformed through the process of production – things like natural beauty, views, sites of spiritual and cultural significance, wilderness, recreation space and so on).

There are several ways in which the assignment of something to the category of 'artefact' (made by people) rather than 'the natural world' - or to 'land', rather than 'environment'- borders on the arbitrary and is made for instrumental rather than principled reasons:

❑ The 'natural world' is nothing like a state of nature but has been shaped by people over the millennia. Improvements, such as drainage or land reclamation, are treated in a stewardship economy as gradually decaying in value until they can be considered to have become part of the natural world. This does not have to do with 'naturalness' but with the ownership claims that people can reasonably have.

☐ I do not include cultivated plants, trees and farm animals as part of the 'natural world' or 'the environment' but as 'artefacts'. This is not intended to diminish their status as living beings but because it is appropriate for farmers to own these beings in a stewardship economy.

☐ The distinction between 'people' and 'the natural world' may also seem false. We are all part of nature. Why distinguish between, say, a dam made by a beaver and a dam made by humans? The reason that I do so is to make it easier for us humans to sort out our thinking about our property claims to the natural world. Beavers have other ways of dealing with property.

☐ A small stream flowing through a plot of land, used only by the steward of that land, is considered to be part of that land. A river flowing through a plot of land, to which others have rights to abstract water, to travel, to fish and so on, is considered to be part of a network of water resources and so to be part of the environment. The classification of a larger stream is made by a regulatory body according to agreed criteria.

Rent

I use the word **'rent'** to refer to regular **payments made for the use of any part of the natural world, particularly for the use of land**.

This differs from the way the term is used in an everyday and commercial sense, where the 'rent' of a property includes both *rent* for the use of land (the plot of ground, or site) and *rental* for the improvements (the bricks and mortar).

It also differs from the way that the term is used by economists. They apply the term 'economic rent', or just plain 'rent', not just to payments made for the use of land and the natural world but for anything that is scarce and cannot be produced in larger quantities at will (that is fixed in supply). So, they use the term 'rent' to refer to payments for a rare painting, the use of a patent or intellectual property, or a unique opera singer. They also refer to the super-normal profits that occur where there is imperfect competition as 'rent'(Robert Kuttner 1999:27). I restrict the use of rent to payments for the use of land and the environment, not to people (even when their contribution is unique) or artefacts (even where these are fixed in supply). So, I restrict rent to payments for the use of the natural world or, as Fred Harrison and James Robertson say, 'payments that people make for what they take from the value of common resources'.

Market rent

The 'market rent' of a plot of land, of a property comprising land and improvements such as buildings or of an aspect of the environment is the 'estimated amount for which a property should lease (let) on the date of valuation between a willing lessor and a willing lessee on appropriate lease terms in an arms-length transaction after proper marketing wherein the parties had each acted knowledgeably, prudently and without compulsion' (RICS 2009:42). The market rent reflects the potential revenue from land when it is put to its highest and best permissible use and is not necessarily related to the rent that is being paid for its current use.

In the context of stewardship, the appropriate lease terms refer to land or the environment but not to buildings and improvements; and include an indefinite duration, annual reviews, annual payments (as monthly instalments) and liability for any damage, pollution or other disimprovement to the land or environment.

It is easiest to determine the market rent of a plot of land when it has no buildings or other improvements on it. When the rent of unimproved land is established by offering it to the highest bidder in the open market, this sale determines the market rent of the land.

'Market rent 'is also used to apply to a resource rent of some aspect of the environment – for example the spectrum auctions revealed the market rent, or resource rent, of those parts of the electromagnetic spectrum.

Market value

The 'market value' – of a plot of land, of a property comprising land and improvements such as buildings or of an aspect of the environment – is the 'estimated amount for which a property should *exchange* on the date of valuation between a willing seller and a willing buyer in an arms-length transaction after proper marketing wherein the parties had each acted knowledgeably, prudently and without compulsion'.

True cost

I use the term 'true cost' of something to an individual or firm to mean the sum of the private costs (direct cost to them) and the external costs (costs borne by others, by society or by the environment). Economists call the true cost the 'social cost'.

Stewardship

The term steward is thought to be derived from 'sty-ward', a person who looks after farm animals. It has been consistently used to mean 'one who manages the affairs of an estate on behalf of his employer'. 'Stewardship' has been used more generally to describe a responsible approach to managing something on behalf of others – for example, a conservationist approach to the natural world, a sense of responsibility to other people, other species, future generations, God.

Many people would think of stewardship as managing the natural world on behalf of something greater than just humankind. 'Dark Greens' recognise our responsibility not just to humankind but to all living things and to Gaia herself – because they recognise that we are not separate from nature, but part of it (Ralph Metzner

1995:66). People of faith may understand this responsibility in recognition of God's dominion over the world and the universe.

Each of these groups come to the word 'stewardship' with rather different assumptions. And the term is used with other meanings in other contexts. For example, Christians also use it to describe something quite different – the practice of tithing a proportion of income to the church. And the UK Department for Environment, Food and Rural Affairs (Defra) and Natural England administer an Environmental Stewardship Scheme that makes payments to farmers who protect and enhance the natural environment.

Nick Dennys (2002: 14) points out that if we are to bring about stewardship we need to celebrate, value and protect the environment; and that democracy in valuation requires the use of market valuations. He advocates the return of this value to the community.

The steward of a part of the natural world has:
- the right of access – to use it in the way that they choose, within the constraints of any relevant regulations
- the responsibility of care – to manage it responsibly and husband it for future generations, accepting liability for any damage done to it
- the duty of compensation – to pay an annual fee, equal to its market rent, into a fund that is used to benefit everyone.
- ownership, in the conventional sense, of any buildings or other improvements.

We do not and cannot own the Earth but can, and must, act as its steward.

Stewardship, then, is a very particular form of private property rights – a relationship between people and the whole of the natural world, not just the parts that might be deemed worthy of conservation.

'Green' versions of stewardship insist that our responsibility is to all living things, both now and for ever. 'Brown' versions are more likely to discount our responsibility to other species and to future generations.

Stewardship fee

A stewardship fee is an annual fee that is paid to secure the stewardship of a plot of land, equal to its market rent.

A stewardship fee is a charge on the market rent of land. If the revenue were to be used as revenue for the state, it would be not a fee or charge but a Land Value Tax. Supporters of Land Value Taxation from time to time question whether the term conveys its intended meaning in the 21st century (Robert Andelson: 2000:xxiii). I prefer 'stewardship' for several reasons:

'Land Value Taxation 'is used to refer to the collection of *any* proportion of the market rent of land – and people are usually talking about less than 25 per cent. I use 'stewardship', on the other hand, to describe the collection of 100 per cent of the market rent. It is helpful to have a term that always refers to this most radical end of the Land Value Tax spectrum – both because some supporters of Land Value Taxation would distance themselves from stewardship, which they think is too extreme to be of practical interest, and because methods of valuation that work well when less than 50 per cent of the market rent is collected cannot be used in a stewardship economy.

'Stewardship fee 'avoids several other possible confusions that accompany the term Land Value Taxation. One is that it avoids any confusion about the meaning of the term 'land'. Another is that the word 'value' seems to suggest to many people that the land itself has an intrinsic value, probably because the term 'Land Value Taxation 'was introduced at a time when the agricultural sector was of much greater economic importance, markets for produce were more local and the 'original and indestructible powers of the soil' were as important as its location.

'Stewardship fee' also has the advantage of avoiding the word 'tax', which should be reserved to mean 'income derived by the sovereign or state from its subjects or citizens'. The precise demarcation between a tax and a charge (or fee) may be contested, but the special characteristic of a tax is that it is unrelated to any specific benefit provided by the state; while a charge, or fee, is a payment for receiving some identifiable benefit. A stewardship fee is a charge for the right, conferred by the state on the steward, to use a specific plot of land or an aspect of the environment for a defined length of time. Although part of the revenue from stewardship fees may provide income for the state, the rest is distributed as a Universal Income.

Most importantly, the term 'stewardship' emphasises that this is more than just a different way of raising revenue. It is an entirely different property system – private property without private ownership .

Universal Income

An essential feature of stewardship is that the stewardship fees are pooled and used for the benefit of all, either as government revenue or as a small independent income in the form of a Universal Income that is distributed to everybody.

Rather than using the term 'Citizen's Income' or 'Basic Income' in the context of stewardship, I refer to a Universal Income. This is in part because I want to emphasise the universal and unconditional entitlement rather than become bogged down in the inevitably exclusive definitions of citizenship and limitations to entitlement. It is mainly, however, because discussions about Citizen's Income and Basic Income have tended to focus on an income funded from conventional taxation, while I am referring to a potentially more generous income that is available when some of the revenue from stewardship fees is available as a source of funding. Universal Income is not to be confused with the very different benefit proposed by the coalition government, the Universal Credit.

Stewardship economy

A stewardship economy is one in which the natural world is held in stewardship, and things made by people are held in ownership.

In a stewardship economy the income from stewardship fees may be used instead of conventional taxes as a source of revenue for the state; or distributed to the whole population as a Universal Income. The income from environmental charges is distributed on an equal per capita basis as Environmental Dividend or invested for the benefit of future generations.

References

Andelson, Robert (ed) (2000) *Land value taxation around the world* Oxford Blackwells

Barnes, Peter (2001) *Who owns the sky?: our common assets and the future of capitalism* Washington Island Press

Basic Income Grant Coalition (2009) *Making the difference! The BIG in Namibia* www.bignam.org NANGOF

Coase, Ronald (1959) *The Federal Communications Commission* Journal of Law and Economics *2* 1-40

Dennys, Nick (2002) Land and Liberty Summer 14

Douglas, Clifford Hugh (1924) *Social Credit* London Cecil Palmer

Galbraith, John Kenneth (1987) *A history of economics* Hamish Hamilton

Galbraith, John Kenneth (1992) *The culture of contentment* London Sinclair-Stevenson

George, Henry (1879) *Progress and poverty* San Francisco Wm M Hinton

Harrison, Fred (2006a) *Wheels of fortune* London Institute of Economic Affairs

Harrison, Fred (2006b) *Ricardo's Law: house prices and the great tax clawback scam* London Shepheard-Walwyn

Harrison, Fred (2008) *The silver bullet* London The International Union for Land Value Taxation

Huber, Joseph & Robertson, James (2000) *Creating new money: a monetary reform for the information age* London New Economics Foundation

Hudson, Michael (2000) *Mesopotamia and Classical Antiquity* in Robert Andelson

Hyndman, Henry (1911) *The record of an adventurous life* London MacMillan

Jacobs, Jane (1992) *Systems of survival: a dialogue on the moral foundations of commerce and politics* New York Random House

Johnson, Robb (2000) *6B go swimming* in Margaret Thatcher: my part in her downfall Irregular Records

Kuttner, Robert (1999) *Everything for sale: the virtues and limits of markets* Chicago University of Chicago Press

Lanchester, John (2010) *Whoops!: why everyone owes everyone and no one can pay* London Allen Lane

Lukes, Steven (1974) *Power: a radical view* London Macmillan

MacDonald, James (2000) *Licence to call* Economist 3/6/2000:6

Mamdani, Mahmood (2011) *The invention of the indigène* London Review of Books *33 (2) (20/1/11)* 31-33

McBurney, Stuart (1990) *Ecology into economics won't go* Bideford Green Books

Metzner, Ralph (1995) *The psychopathology of the human-nature relationship* in Theodore Rozak

Mill, John Stuart (1848) *Principles of political economy with their applications to social philosophy* London John Parker

Mirrlees, James et al (2011) *Tax by design: the Mirrlees Review* Oxford www.ifs.org.uk/mirrleesreview (draft)

Paine, Thomas (1797a) *Agrarian Justice* London T G Ballard

Parker, Hermione (1989) *Instead of the dole: an enquiry into the integration of the tax and benefit systems* London Routledge

Ricardo, David (1817) *On the principles of political economy, and taxation (Vol 1)* London John Murray

RICS (2006) *Valuation Information Paper 9: land and building apportionments for lease classification under international financial reporting standards* London Royal Institute of Chartered Surveyors

RICS (2009) *RICS Valuation standards (Red book)* London Royal Institute of Chartered Surveyors

Robertson, James (1994) *Benefits and taxes: a radical strategy* London New Economics Foundation

Roche, Barbara (1998) *Written answer to parliamentary question 18th May* London Hansard

Roszak, Theodore; Gomes, Mary & Kanner, Allen (eds) (1995) *Ecopsychology: Restoring the earth, healing the mind* San Francisco Sierra Club Books

Samuelson, Paul & Nordhaus, William (1992 (14th edition)) *Economics* New York McGraw-Hill

Smith, Adam (1776) *An inquiry into the nature and causes of the wealth of nations* Dublin Whitestone et al.

Spence, Thomas (1775a) *A lecture read at the philosophical society in Newcastle , on Nov the 8th, 1775* in Thomas Spence 1796

Spence, Thomas (1796) *The meridian sun of liberty; or, the whole rights of man displayed, and most accurately defined* London Thomas Spence

Steiner, Hillel (1994) *An essay on rights* Oxford Blackwell

Stewart, John (2010) *Prime minister* London Shepheard-Walwyn

Torry, Malcolm (2009) *Can unconditional cash transfers work? They can* Citizen's Income Trust Newsletter *2*

Townsend, Peter & Davidson, Nick (eds) (1982) *Inequalities in health: the Black report* London Pelican

Vickers, Tony (2007) *Location matters: recycling Britain's wealth* London Shepheard-Walwyn

Wadsworth, Mark (2006) *Tax, benefits, pensions: keep it simple Part 2: ten steps to simplicity* www.bowgroup.org/content.asp?pageid=5

Winstanley, Gerrard (Jerard Winstanly)) (1649) *A watch word to the City of London and the army* London Calvert

About the Author

Julian Pratt (1948-2018) grew up in London, and, as a young doctor in 1975, he went to rural South Africa. It was here he questioned the factors contributing to the pattern of disease and realised how the grossly unequal distribution of land for agriculture was having a devastating effect on people's health, the consequences of poverty, malnutrition and the need for migrant labour.

As a result of this experience, Julian became passionate about land reform and pursued this interest for the next 40 years. He researched, proposed and campaigned for a radical approach to the market economy, one which would replace private ownership of land with a system he described as stewardship.

Following his time in Africa, Julian became a GP in Sheffield, job-sharing with Rosemary, his wife, and working from new surgery premises, the UK's first super-insulated non-residential building. Increasingly interested in systems of care, in 1993 Julian moved to the King's Fund in London, a health policy think tank. He wrote a book, Practitioners and Practices: A Conflict of Values? (1995) and with colleagues developed a "whole system" approach to improving healthcare which drew on complexity theory and viewed organisations as living systems.

After 2011, when he published Stewardship Economy, he continued to research the ideas and write the substantial body of work that lies behind it. He made presentations to meetings and organised conferences on the topic with special interest groups, in academic settings and to wider audiences, gathering questions raised to inform the writing of his books.

www.ingramcontent.com/pod-product-compliance
Lightning Source LLC
Chambersburg PA
CBHW051213170526
45166CB00005B/1868